Murder At Broad River Bridge

by Bill Shipp

With a foreword by Renee C. Romano
With a new preface to the paperback edition

◆

The University of Georgia Press
Athens, Georgia

Published by the University of Georgia Press
Athens, Georgia 30602
www.ugapress.org
Copyright © 1981 by Bill Shipp
Additional materials © 2017 by the University of Georgia Press
All rights reserved

Most University of Georgia Press titles are
available from popular e-book vendors.

Printed digitally

Library of Congress Cataloging-in-Publication Data
Names: Shipp, Bill, author. | Romano, Renee Christine, writer of foreword.
Title: Murder at Broad River Bridge : the slaying of Lemuel Penn by the Ku
    Klux Klan / by Bill Shipp ; with a foreword by Renee C. Romano ; with a
    new preface to the paperback edition.
Description: Athens : The University of Georgia Press, [2017] | Originally
    published: Atlanta, Ga. : Peachtree Publishers, 1981.
Identifiers: LCCN 2017020940| ISBN 9780820351612 (pbk. : alk. paper) | ISBN
9780820351629 (ebook)
Subjects: LCSH: Ku Klux Klan (1915-)—Georgia. | Penn, Lemuel. | Murder—
Georgia—Athens.
Classification: LCC HS2330.K63 S48 2017 | DDC 364.152/3092 [B]—dc23
LC record available at https://lccn.loc.gov/2017020940

Originally published by Peachtree Publishers, LTD in 1981

To my loving wife Reny
for her enduring patience.

In addition, I wish to thank my friends and
colleagues, Hal Gulliver and Dick Kattel, for their
counseling and encouragement in this project.

CONTENTS

With special acknowledgement
to retired FBI Agent Jack B. Simpson
for his invaluable assistance in
research for this story.

FOREWORD

ON JULY 11, 1964, shortly after 4 a.m. on a narrow Georgia highway, Lemuel Penn became yet another victim of racial violence during the tense years of the civil rights struggle in the South. Penn, a forty-nine-year-old assistant superintendent of the Washington, D.C., schools, had been in Georgia for two weeks for active army reserve training at Fort Benning. As he was driving back home with two other African American army reservists, three local Ku Klux Klansman saw the car with Washington, D.C., license plates and decided the black men inside—who they thought might have been "President Johnson's boys" sent down South to "stir up trouble"—needed to be taught a lesson. Two quick shotgun blasts into the car left Lemuel Penn dead. But this time the Klansmen targeted the wrong victim—a reserve soldier not involved in any civil rights protests, whose only "crime" had been coming to Georgia for mandatory training. The federal government almost immediately stepped in, leading to an investigation and legal process that would eventually begin to curb the power of the Klan. In *Murder at Broad River Bridge*, veteran journalist Bill Shipp tells this powerful story of Lemuel Penn's death, of a Klan run rampant in the South, and of a federal government finally taking action to rein in racially motivated violence.

Lemuel Penn was only one among hundreds of blacks who were murdered during the 1950s and 1960s in a last-ditch effort to protect the system of white supremacy in the South. In fact, no one knows for sure how many African Americans and their white allies were killed during the civil rights era. Victims included leaders of the civil rights struggle like Medgar Evers, who was gunned down in front of his home in Jackson, Mississippi, in 1963; black and white civil rights volunteers and foot soldiers such as James Chaney, Mickey Schwerner, Andrew Goodman, and Viola Liuzzo; and many blacks, like Lemuel Penn, who were not actively involved in protests but whose deaths were intended as a form of terrorism designed to uphold the racial status quo.

While most of the killings of the civil rights era were committed by a relatively few men, most of whom were in the Ku Klux Klan, *Murder at Broad River Bridge* begins to make clear that the Klan could only operate so brazenly because of the complicity of the larger community. Shipp tells us of white leaders in Athens, Georgia, who refused to cooperate with the FBI investigation into Penn's murder and journalists who refused to cover local black protests against a popular segregated drive-in restaurant. In many other communities where murders took place, white business and religious leaders hesitated to openly condemn Klan violence, political elites blamed bombings and murders on "outside agitators" or described them as hoaxes meant to win sympathy for civil rights protestors, and the larger white community closed ranks around alleged perpetrators once crimes drew outside media and political attention. When the two men who killed Emmett Till in Mississippi in 1955 were charged with the crime, every single defense lawyer in the county volunteered to work on their behalf. When Byron de la Beckwith was released after a mistrial in the 1963 shooting of Medgar Evers, he was welcomed home with a parade. This kind of public support of the white community enabled violent white resistance to flourish.

The complicity of the broader white society was reflected most dramatically in the near-complete failure of the justice system to protect the lives of blacks. In the Jim Crow South, many policemen belonged to the Klan, and nearly all of them saw it as their mission to uphold and protect segregation and white supremacy. Southern law enforcement condoned and enabled Klan violence by refusing to investigate bombings, beatings, and acts of arson. As in the case of the men who killed Lemuel Penn, the failure of police to intervene when Klansmen openly terrorized or intimidated local blacks only emboldened more violence. Shipp sardonically notes that police in Athens, Georgia, may have had their hands full trying to contain an active Klan chapter in 1964. They proved a rather "obliging lot" who freely offered the Klan information, looked the other way when Klansmen publicly threatened blacks, and even traded firearms with them.

The broader criminal justice system proved obliging too. Even though Joseph Howard Sims and Cecil Myers, two of the Klansmen involved in Lemuel Penn's murder, were put on trial on murder charges by the state of Georgia in 1964, they—like most other white men accused of racially motivated murders in the segregated South—had little to fear from a jury of their peers. Defense attorneys for Sims and Myers argued that Klan violence helped maintain racial order and thus benefitted the entire white community. Jurors, the defense argued, should remember their own "Anglo-Saxon heritage" and do their duty to protect the two accused men from an overreaching federal government that sought to sacrifice the southern way of life. It took the jury all of three hours of deliberation to find Sims and Myers not guilty. After watching a jury acquit the men who beat Reverend James Reeb to death in 1965 because he had come to Alabama to participate in a voting rights march, Unitarian minister Walter Jones warned that "murder is not murder except in the community that regards it as so." Most communities in the South, like that in Athens, Georgia, did not regard these racially motivated killings as murders that deserved legal punishment.

If *Murder at Broad River Bridge* provides a cautionary tale of both the dangers of an unchecked Ku Klux Klan and of the failure of communities and especially of the legal system to protect black lives, Bill Shipp finds some hope in the actions the federal government took to demand justice in this case. Lemuel Penn's murder led to a quick and effective federal response. The FBI arrived shortly after the murder and launched an impressive investigation that swiftly identified the key suspects. Federal authorities sought to aid the state of Georgia in its prosecution of Penn's accused killers. When a state jury acquitted Sims and Myers, the Department of Justice went to court to argue that it had the jurisdiction to try Klansmen like them on federal charges of conspiring to violate the civil rights of their victims. When the Supreme Court sided with the Justice Department, federal prosecutors pointed to Penn's murder to charge Myers, Sims, and four other Klansmen with engaging in "a broad conspiracy to keep out-of-state Negroes from coming into the Athens area." While a federal jury acquitted four of the men, Myers and Sims were found guilty and sentenced to ten years in jail, which was the maximum sentence possible on a conspiracy charge.

But while the FBI and Department of Justice acted decisively in this case, the singular story of Penn's murder and its aftermath told in *Murder at Broad River Bridge* can obscure the much longer story of federal foot-dragging and inaction in response to racially motivated violence. Indeed, from the perspective of civil rights activists, the federal government until the mid-1960s was more a part of the problem than it was a useful ally or protector. The federal government proved unwilling to take meaningful action to protect black Americans from racial terrorism for most of the civil rights era. Even when the FBI seriously investigated some civil rights–era murders, their investigations rarely led to any prosecutions or served to prevent further racial violence. "There is no substitute under the federal system for the failure of local law enforcement," Assistant Attorney General Burke Marshall declared in 1963, and for many civil rights activists, the image of an FBI agent quietly observing and taking notes while white mobs beat up protestors was far more accurate than that of dutiful federal agents taking the steps necessary to protect black lives. It was unrestrained Klan violence that finally forced the federal government's hand; officials came to realize that they would have to intervene in order to maintain any kind of legal order in the South and to protect America's democratic image around the world. But the Penn case marked a dramatic turning point in ways that a short book focused specifically on that case cannot always communicate.

If this book has much to teach us about the history of Klan violence in the 1960s, the decision by the University of Georgia Press to reissue it in 2017 offers another kind of history lesson. South African Archbishop Desmond Tutu has famously described certain pasts as "refusing to lie down quietly." Racially motivated murders in the 1950s and 1960s tore communities apart. They revealed state complicity with racial violence and the almost complete failure of the legal system to protect and value black lives. Histories that reflect unresolved systemic violence, as Tutu suggests, often refuse to become history.

In the years since Bill Shipp's book was first published in 1981, the racial violence of the civil rights era has made insistent claims upon the present to be remembered and to be redressed. Since the mid-1990s, many states have faced pressure to reopen and bring criminal

charges in cold civil rights–era murder cases. In the past two decades, hundreds of these cases have been reinvestigated, and more than
twenty men have been convicted and sentenced to jail time for racial
murders committed decades earlier. Even in Athens, Georgia, where
Lemuel Penn's killers were eventually meted out some punishment,
Penn's murder has refused to "lie down quietly." In 2004, community
members concerned that people in the Athens area had forgotten the
story of this crime formed a memorial committee to raise money to
put up a historical marker at the site where Penn was shot. Such a
marker was necessary, one supporter argued, because if people didn't
understand the past, they would be more likely to repeat it.

And now, more than ever, we need to learn the lessons that Penn's
story can teach us. The reissuing of *Murder at Broad River Bridge* is
especially timely in 2017 as it reflects the stark truth that the racial violence of the civil rights era continues to have lessons and legacies for
the present day. Articulated by the Black Lives Matter Movement, the
response to the many recent killings of unarmed black men, women,
and children makes clear that the criminal justice system all too frequently treats black lives as less valuable than others. Shipp's book can
help us to see that it takes commitment and political work to make
sure that the criminal justice system treats everyone equally. It is an
ongoing and vital project.

Renee C. Romano

PREFACE to the Paperback Edition: Past and Present

WHEN A RESURGENT KU KLUX KLAN and their allies rode wild across the land in the 1950s and 1960s, some of us believed they embodied the last vestiges of the American Civil War. Some even dared hope that the day of the night riders and other mongers of racial terror in the South would soon end.

The population of the South has expanded and diversified. Time has created a distance from the bitter days of Reconstruction. Leaders of the newest New South predicted loudly that the Klan and their ilk would shortly go the way of the dinosaur. So when the old lizards vanished, we were not prepared for their successors. In the old days, the KKK crowd was heavily nationalistic, with many of its members having served in the military of World War II, the Korean War, and Vietnam. Many were proud to call themselves part of the so-called Greatest Generation. Blind as they were to the coming tide of change, the old racists were certain they held the keys to a better day—a day when reawakened America would adopt their old brand of white supremacy.

Their progeny harbored no such naïve belief in a coming brighter time. These folks were dedicated to wrecking Western democracy and its venerable institutions. They vowed to install a new level of white authoritarianism and restore a discriminatory social infrastructure. Whereas their fathers and grandfathers saw America as a shining city on the mountaintop, a venue that embodied Christian virtue and knightly codes of conduct, their children scoffed at such notions. Instead, the new crowd that inherited the "greatest" mantle pushed aside their inheritance. They strove to build a society of chaos—one that would be owned and operated by a lily-white kakistocracy of antidemocrats.

For the sake of brevity and clarity, we will not refer to these new rebels as millennials, alt-right, or anything else of that kind. Instead, let us discuss these first inhabitants of the twenty-first century for what they are. They are mostly, in the South, part of the current generation.

Their moral code is far different from that of their forebearers. Both generations believed, or at least said they believed, in white supremacy. But the modern lot saw more than just white superiority; instead they envisioned a new age of white dominance and Big Brother governments throughout much of the world.

I don't write this to lay out a forecast of the future; rather, I have come to outline a tragic calamity of the past, a violent dying gasp of the American Civil War and the hatred that the conflict spawned: the murder of Lemuel Penn by members of the KKK. Many of us hoped that this dark incident included a tiny silver lining for a new and better day in which, through changing hearts and civil and legal protection, there might be a dawn of a new day of hope and happiness among all races. Alas, our assessment may have been wrong. The violent death of Penn may have been a simple harbinger that the worst was yet to come and that violence such as Penn's shooting death would soon become a common occurrence. Racism prevails on our streets more than ever. Here, then, for your edification and guidance, is the Penn story.

Murder At Broad River Bridge

◆

PROLOGUE "Protectors of Our Children"

THE KU KLUX KLAN started as a social club of Confederate veterans in Pulaski, Tennessee, in 1866, just after the Civil War. Less than a year later, the organization was restructured at a meeting in Nashville, Tennessee, along the lines of white supremacy. It became "The Invisible Empire of the South."

Within two years, the robed and hooded Klansmen were riding the backroads of the South, whipping and killing in acts of terrorism aimed at restoring white supremacy. They served on juries, too, unrecognized, and they posted placards threatening blacks and whites alike, bullying any whose ways did not suit the Klan.

The number of kidnappings and murders increased to such an alarming extent that new federal laws were passed, and the grand wizard of the Klan himself ordered the organization disbanded in 1869. Local groups paid little attention to that call, continuing to operate with vigilante disregard for any law but their own. They still operate that way.

In June of 1979, a neatly dressed, articulate young man spoke to a crowd in Euless, Texas. His name was David Duke, age twenty-eight, of Metairie, Louisiana. This college-educated young man looked and acted much like an up-and-coming Southern politician. He was, in fact, one of the new leaders of the Ku Klux Klan, which experienced new vitality as the decade of the 1970s ended and the decade of the 1980s began.

"The general Hollywood-New York axis doesn't oppose us because of our robes but primarily because of our beliefs," Duke told the crowd in Euless.

Duke and the current crop of wizards, dragons, and cyclopses like to tell their audiences that Klan violence is a myth perpetuated by the hostile federal government and militant black leaders. They contend nightriding and lynchings went out of style fifty years ago.

On the day Duke spoke in Texas, Klansmen forced the public swimming pools to close in Selma, Alabama. Mayor Joe Smitherman said he was ordering the pools closed to avoid violence after

3

robed Klansmen appeared at one pool, saying they were there "to protect the children."

Three weeks earlier, four men had been wounded by gunfire at a confrontation between Klansmen and black demonstrators in Decatur, Alabama.

"The Ku Klux Klan is growing all over the country," says Duke. He, like the other new wizards of the hooded order, claims that the new Klan will aid "white people" through political pressure and public relations.

Klansmen of the 1960s sang the same tune. Georgia Grand Dragon Calvin Craig of the United Klans of America publicly espoused political action as the Klan strategy. Meanwhile, blacks were killed and maimed all across the South. Klansmen put to the torch homes and churches where civil rights demonstrations and voter registration projects were planned.

Do not be misled by the likes of David Duke. The Ku Klux Klan is not a political action committee. The essence of the Klan is not to be found in its mumbo-jumbo system of lodge-hall officialdom or in its juvenile secret jargon. The essence of the so-called "Klanskraft" is fear and violence. Today's Klansmen are underground fighters on the wrong side of a war against oppression and lawlessness. Today's Klansmen are no different from the armed hoodlums of yesteryear who murdered and destroyed in the name of white supremacy.

That is why it is worth remembering this true story of how the Klan prospered and thrived on violence in the city of Athens, Georgia, in the 1960s, while the townspeople looked on in apathy and sometimes encouraged the hooded thugs in their vicious doings — until an innocent stranger was murdered on a lonely road in the dark of night.

This is the story of events surrounding the slaying of Lemuel Penn. Penn was only one victim of the Klan in the South in 1964. Perhaps recalling a single tragic episode and some of the occurrences before and after his murder will remind us of that era so that we will not have to endure such shame again — and so that when the David Dukes speak and the robed "protectors of our children" appear, we will know them for what they are.

BILL SHIPP

1 • Trouble Back up the Road

THIS STORY BEGINS ON JULY 10, 1964.

The nation was trying to pull itself back together after the shattering murder of a president in Dallas only a few months before. The late president's brother, Robert Kennedy, was still attorney general of the United States, although he would soon leave the cabinet to seek a U.S. Senate seat from New York. President Lyndon Johnson was at the height of his personal popularity. The war in Vietnam was a factor, but a minor one, on the American political landscape. It was not yet perceived as a bitterly divisive involvement that would split the American people and undercut Johnson's presidency. Johnson, that long hot summer, was perceived very much as a strong leader, a white Southerner who had aggressively pushed through Congress the civil rights legislation first introduced by the late John Kennedy. Johnson was an experienced man who had proven himself capable of being president after the tragedy in Dallas. He would be rewarded that fall with a landslide election victory.

Neither Lyndon Johnson nor Robert Kennedy knew it on that July 10, but both would have roles to play in the turmoil that followed the death of Lemuel Penn. Both Johnson and Kennedy

5

ordered the full resources of the Department of Justice and the FBI brought into play in solving the Penn slaying.

Penn himself had every personal reason to feel good that day, despite his forty-nine years and receding hairline and the beginnings of a paunch. He had just spent two long but uneventful weeks of active army reserve training at Fort Benning, near Columbus, Georgia, and now he was ready to put aside his lieutenant colonel's uniform with the rows of ribbons on the left breast and get back home, back to his family and job in Washington, D.C.

The drive home, in a fellow officer's car, would be long and arduous. He wanted to feel comfortable. He dressed in a blue sports shirt, tan flannel pants, and a pair of brown oxfords. He fastened his gold Omega watch around his left wrist and placed his 1957 Phelps Vocational High School gold ring with the blue stone on the fourth finger of his left hand. He carefully cleaned his plastic-rimmed glasses and fitted them snugly over his nose and ears. The glasses case was clipped to his belt on the right side. It was almost midnight when he was ready to leave.

Life had been good to Penn lately. He had few complaints. He was in good health despite some old gall-bladder problems. He expected to complete his doctorate in education in a few months. For the past two years he had been an assistant superintendent of schools in charge of vocational and adult education in the District of Columbia.

He had taught in the District of Columbia school system for twenty years, taking time out for World War II. He could recall his first teaching job in the District school system in 1939, when the system was segregated and there were limited opportunities for blacks. During World War II he had seen combat in the South Pacific. When he came home, he remained active in the army reserve. He rose to the rank of lieutenant colonel.

Penn was an energetic and ambitious man. Besides directing the District's five vocational schools, he was placed in charge of evening and summer classes and handled most personnel matters for vocational and evening schools. He also was active in his Methodist church and in the Boy Scouts. He held the Silver Beaver Award, scouting's highest recognition for leadership. He had organized a scout camp for underprivileged black youths.

Friends said he enjoyed his family. While on reserve duty, he regularly phoned his wife, Georgia, a home economics teacher in the District system. And he liked to chat with his children — Linda, age thirteen; Sharon, age ten; and Lemuel, age five.

Friends also said Penn went out of his way to avoid trouble. And trouble for a black man in the summer of 1964 was easy to find. The civil rights movement was at its height. The Ku Klux Klan also had come back to life to try to counter the black struggle for equal rights.

Lemuel Penn wanted no part of that fight at that time and place. He had other plans for his life. He did not even belong to a civil rights organization. He told his wife by telephone on Thursday night, July 9, that he had not left Fort Benning during his two weeks of active duty. He said he wanted to avoid any possible brush with "racial unpleasantness."

Penn may have sensed that trouble loomed ahead on his trip homeward. Just before checking out of Fort Benning, Penn asked a mess sergeant if an army cook could prepare a lunch for him and his two Washington-bound companions because, Penn said, the three black officers would "probably have some problems" if they tried to use public eating facilities on the way home. The mess sergeant refused Penn's request. It was against regulations, the sergeant explained later.

Shortly after midnight on July 11, 1964, a Chevrolet sedan belonging to reserve officer Charles E. Brown pulled out of the gate at Fort Benning and headed northeast toward Atlanta. Brown's passengers were Lemuel Penn and John D. Howard. All three men were teachers in the District of Columbia school system. Brown and Penn were good personal friends and frequently played bridge together; Penn had known Howard casually since 1938, but they were not especially close.

Howard had first intended to fly back to Washington, but at the last minute canceled his reservations and decided to ride back in Brown's car.

The three-hour trip up Georgia 85 was uneventful in those quiet early-morning hours. Conversation soon trailed off into silence.

When they reached Atlanta, they pulled into a Texaco station and filled up. There Penn unfolded a map to try to find a shorter, less traveled route through Georgia to South Carolina. He found Highway 72 out of Athens, intersecting with Highway 172, which would take them to Hartwell on the South Carolina line. None of the three men had traveled that route through northeast Georgia before. But it looked like a good shortcut. They agreed to take it.

The two state routes went through no major towns and appeared on the map to be primary highways. They were, in fact, narrow, deserted two-lane roads.

The men drove out the then-unfinished Interstate 85 to the Lawrenceville cutoff and swung over to U.S. 29 for the remainder of the sixty-five mile trip to Athens.

It was shortly after 3:30 A.M. when they arrived in Athens. Brown had been driving since Fort Benning and was beginning to feel weary. His fatigue probably saved his life.

Brown pulled the car over and parked on Broad Street in Athens, near the base of a marble and granite monument memorializing Confederate war dead. The car was only a few feet from the ancient arch that is the gateway to the University of Georgia. Lemuel Penn offered to relieve Brown and drive for a while. Brown moved to the right front passenger seat, and Penn took the wheel as they continued through Athens.

None of them noticed three other men in a cream-colored Chevy II station wagon that dropped a couple of hundred yards behind the Penn car as it turned onto Georgia Highway 72 and moved northward out of town.

It was now shortly before 4:00 A.M., Saturday, July 11.

Brown was weary after his driving stint and dozed off. Howard remained awake. But there was not much conversation.

The car moved through the tiny town of Colbert in northeast Georgia. Like any number of small towns in that part of the state, Colbert was closed down at that time of morning. Only the night policeman, Billy Smith, age thirty-six, was on duty. He saw the Penn vehicle pass through town. It was going too fast, he thought, and he started to stop the car for speeding. But the car was not being driven recklessly and there was no other traffic. He decided to let it go on.

Officer Smith was trying to do this job in a proper fashion, including giving a passing motorist the benefit of the doubt. If the night policeman in Colbert had stopped the car, even briefly and only to give a warning, it might have saved Lemuel Penn's life.

Later, Officer Smith said he did not recall seeing the Chevy II station wagon that followed the Penn car. There may have been another car, he said. He just couldn't be certain.

Just outside Colbert, Penn turned left onto Highway 172 on the final leg of the backroad shortcut. The pursuing station wagon began to close. None of the three men in the sedan noticed. Penn rounded a curve and started down a long hill that led to the concrete bridge over the Broad River.

The station wagon suddenly pulled beside them. There were two loud explosions. Brown awoke with a start, thinking for an instant that two blowouts had occurred.

The car swerved crazily and banged into the bridge rail, then bounced back onto the highway. Brown looked up just in time to see the taillights on the station wagon disappear ahead in the fog.

Penn's head slumped forward, his glasses dangling from one ear. His hands dropped from the steering wheel. Brown and Howard both reached out to hold Penn and grab control of the runaway car. Brown felt something warm trickle down his arm. It was blood. The left side of Lemuel Penn's face had been blown away by buckshot. A second shotgun blast into the side of the vehicle had narrowly missed Brown.

Brown, with Howard struggling to help from the backseat, managed to get the car under control without a wreck that might have taken both their lives.

Both men were terrified as they fought to bring the car to a halt.

The terror was not over. The car from which the murderous shotgun fire had come had driven past them, across the Broad River bridge. Brown and Howard were afraid to continue in that direction. They quickly turned their car around and headed back toward Colbert and Athens. Howard was still in the backseat of the car, Brown recalled later, and thought he could see "light shadows" making a turn in the fog. Was the car with their assailants coming back toward the bridge?

"I kept my eye on the rearview mirror, and I could see the lights were steadily gaining on us," Brown later testified.

The night seemed to have gone. The fog pressing down on the

empty, silent highway added to the eeriness. Brown and Howard crossed a road past a stop sign. Looking back into the fog, Brown thought he again saw car lights coming closer. He asked the time. Howard told him it was 5:15 A.M.

Then a second disaster. "We went on a little farther and the fog got heavy again, and I did not make a turn in the road which later turned out to be the junction of 172 and 72," Brown later testified. The car spun off the road into a ditch near a railroad track.

Now there was a new kind of terror. The car turned over on its side, trapping Brown until Howard could help him from the car and they could scramble up the bank to the highway in hopes of flagging down help. But how could they be sure that the next car along the road was not the car with the nightriders and their shotguns? The night had become a nightmare.

Standing by the car at the edge of the highway, Brown discovered he was covered with Lemuel Penn's blood.

*   *   *

Willie Lankford, an intructor at the University of Georgia, pulled out of his driveway in Athens at 4:25 that morning. He and his wife and son and a nephew were on their way to Mt. Airy, North Carolina, to pick up his daughter. They wanted to get an early start so they could arrive in Mt. Airy around noon.

The fog was thick and messy, and Lankford became confused as he left Athens and drove up Highway 72 toward the little village of Hull. He wanted to find the intersection of Highway 172 and drove slowly into Colbert, trying to find the right turn.

Night policeman Billy Smith was still on duty, and Lankford stopped and asked for help. Smith aimed him in the right direction, explaining that the intersection was about a mile and a half down the road. "You can't miss it," he said.

As Lankford later told the story in court, he got back into his car and headed for the intersection of 72 and 172. It was still foggy. He saw a man waving at him and at first thought he was a hitchhiker. Lankford had no intention of picking up a hitchhiker at that time of the morning; it was still dark, and he had his family with him.

"That man is in trouble," Lankford's wife declared abruptly, just as he went past, found the turn, and turned left. "I believe he is hurt," she said.

What did she mean — in trouble? Lankford wanted to know. Had she seen a wreck or a car? No, she had only seen a man trying to flag somebody down, but she was sure something was wrong.

Lankford made a U-turn and drove back slowly to the scene, this time getting a good look at the man by the side of the highway, a black man drenched with blood. "Help us! We are in trouble!" the man shouted.

Lankford's first thought was that the man might have been in a fight. He did not stop his car but drove back to Colbert, only a minute or two away, and notified Billy Smith. "There is trouble back up the road," he told Smith.

Billy Smith thus became the first law enforcement officer to enter the Lemuel Penn case. He examined the body and talked to Howard and Brown before summoning Madison County Sheriff Dewey Seagraves. It was a case that, before it was over, would involve a governor, judges, the Department of Justice, the FBI, and the White House. Not to mention the white knights of the "invisible empire" who still believed that racism and white supremacy should be maintained as an integral part of the Southern — and, yes, the American — way of life.

2 • Two Simple Reasons for Murder

THE SOUTH seethed in violence and hatred in the mid-1960s. Killings, floggings, burnings and bombings occurred in almost every corner of rural Dixie as black people finally moved deliberately to exercise rights guaranteed them by law.

Some of the atrocities perpetrated against blacks and their white allies made headlines. Most did not. It was not until months and even years later that the public learned of the scope of the terror spread by nightriders in the name of protecting the white race.

Athens, Georgia, seemed an unlikely nesting place for Ku Klux marauders. The city, which had a population of about thirty thousand in 1964, was the home of the University of Georgia. The city fathers boastfully referred to their town by its Chamber of Commerce nickname: "The Classic City of the South." The face of Athens most Georgians saw in the 1960s was shiny, intellectual and energetic. Athens was a town of university students, harried professors and hustling entrepreneurs who already sensed the unprecedented growth that lay ahead for the area. It was a city of oak-lined residential streets and stately antebellum homes located just sixty-five miles east-northeast of Atlanta in the Piedmont farm region of Georgia.

But Athens also was the home of textile plants, cottonseed oil makers and tire cord manufacturers. Those industries gave Athens and environs a slightly different face on close inspection. These industries often thrive on the sweat and brawn of poorly educated and poorly paid white workers, who in 1964 stood on a socioeconomic level only slightly higher than that of blacks, who in Athens lived almost exclusively in public housing or in white-owned slums.

Ignorant and oppressed whites in Athens and elsewhere in the South sensed in the early 1960s that their last claims to superiority were about to be challenged. Simply being white would no longer be enough to give them status and a feeling of superiority over all black men and women.

Two black students were admitted to the University of Georgia in 1961. A riot erupted but was quickly subdued. In the spring of the same year, biracial groups who called themselves Freedom Riders began moving across the South to demand integration of facilities at bus stations. They were attacked by mobs, and some of the riders were arrested. But the barriers of race were beginning to crumble.

In 1962, the Supreme Court ruled that federal courts had the power to reapportion state legislatures. Blacks could no longer be systematically excluded from participating in making the state laws that governed them.

The civil rights movement gained momentum. On August 28, 1963, Dr. Martin Luther King, Jr. led a peaceful demonstration of 200,000 persons in Washington, D.C. A year later he would be awarded the Nobel Peace Prize; five years later he would be dead from an assassin's bullet.

Great strides in the struggle for equal rights were made in 1964. Poll taxes were finally outlawed. Fair and equitable congressional districting was ordered. President Johnson signed the Civil Rights Act, which protected voting rights, prohibited racial discrimination in employment and in public accommodations, and encouraged school desegregation.

Johnson and King both became hated men in the Old Confederacy, and the Ku Klux Klan thrived as never before. There were at least seventeen separate and independent KKK organizations operating in the 1960s in the southeastern United States. At least sixteen thousand men and a few hundred women counted themselves as active adherents to the terroristic principles of the hooded order and the fiery cross.

Most acts of violence directed against blacks and whites in this era of social revolution had a common theme. The Klan viewed its victims as the enemy in a white-black war. Viola Liuzzo, white, was murdered in Alabama in 1965 because she participated in civil rights activities. Michael Schwerner and Andrew Goodman, both white, and James Chaney, black, were kidnapped and murdered by Klansmen in Mississippi in 1964 because they were "agitators" against segregation. Medgar Evers was slain in 1963 by a sniper in Mississippi for his work in the National Association for the Advancement of Colored People. Four black children died in the bombing of a church in Birmingham, Alabama, in 1963. The church was a center for organizing black demonstrations.

Lemuel A. Penn was murdered on a desolate Georgia highway near Athens in the summer of 1964 for different reasons. He did not die because he was an "outside agitator." He was not even a member of a civil rights organization. Lemuel Penn was killed for two reasons: his skin was black and his car bore a District of Columbia license plate.

"We thought he might've been one of President Johnson's boys," a Klansman would say later in a sworn statement to the FBI in explaining why Penn's life was taken.

3 • Weep for the Coward

JULY 11, 1964, was the hardest day Charles E. Brown ever experienced. Even after help arrived at the tragic scene just outside Colbert, there was a new ordeal: rural lawmen poking flashlights into the car and shining them on Penn's body, now lying on the floorboard. "What's been goin' on here?" one officer drawled suspiciously at Brown and Howard. Then came the long hours of questioning, by local officials first, then state officials, and finally federal officials. There seemed to be a tone in the questioning that somehow Penn, Brown and Howard had caused trouble, and that this was their retribution.

But there had been no trouble, not until the sudden shotgun blasts on that desolate road.

Both Howard and Brown were allowed to use telephones in Athens to notify their families. Military authorities were notified at nearby Fort Gordon. Brown and Howard were numb from grief, shock and exhaustion. The hardest telephone call of all was left to Brown, the call to Georgia Penn to tell her that her husband had been murdered in Georgia.

Penn died on a Saturday. On that Sunday and Monday, hundreds of people called on Georgia Penn and the three children to offer condolences at the Penns' neat frame-and-brick home on a tree-shaded street in a quiet, recently desegregated Washington residential area.

"It is a pity that he could live through World War II and not be able to return home and live within the boundaries of his own country in safety and security," Georgia Penn told friends with understandable bitterness.

On Monday evening the coffin was taken to Jones Memorial Methodist Church in Washington and opened so that mourners could view the remains of Lemuel Penn for the last time. Penn had been a trustee of the church.

In an emotional service on Tuesday, the Reverend Stafford Harris told the mourners: "Weep not for this peace-loving man, but weep for the coward who stooped to such a crime. . . . Lemuel Penn now rides for God's battlefields."

Penn was eulogized for his work in education by Carl Hanson, school superintendent for the District of Columbia. A commendation from Penn's military unit was read at the service. It had been prepared while Penn was at Fort Benning and was to have been presented to him upon his return home.

Olaf Slostad, an official of the Boy Scouts of America, an organization in which Penn had been an active and honored leader, read from the pulpit: "On my honor I will do my best to do my duty."

The altar where the body lay was banked with flowers. On a red, white, and blue spray was a card that read: "A magnificent gentleman — from his friends and military associates of the 222nd Maneuver Control Command, Ft. Meade, Maryland." This was from Penn's army reserve unit, the one that had sent him on his fateful journey to Fort Benning that summer.

An army caisson, drawn by six grays, approached the Arlington National Cemetery gravesite to the strains of "Onward Christian Soldiers," played by the army band. The music changed to "Abide With Me" as the casket was lifted over the grave.

The caisson at last stood empty.

It was the same caisson that had carried President John F. Kennedy's body to his grave seven months earlier.

Georgia Penn and her children wept.

Slightly more than a year later, on July 20, 1965, Georgia Penn died at George Washington University Hospital. Doctors attributed her death at forty-nine to a rare form of arthritis. Friends said she never recovered from the shock of her husband's death, and died of a broken heart.

4 • The Governor Makes a Guess

IF CARL SANDERS was a proud man, perhaps he had some right. He had risen from obscurity as a member of the Georgia state Senate to become the first governor of Georgia "elected by all of the people." Prior to the 1962 election, Georgia governors were elected by a county unit system that gave the state's rural counties considerably more political weight than the more populous urban and suburban areas.

Carl Sanders was hailed in the early and mid-1960s as the first of the New South's governors. He was handsome and urbane, considered moderate for his time. There were still racial problems in Georgia, he felt, but the worst was over. He had been elected governor with overwhelming support from black voters. He was politically bold, once appearing on a long network television interview on school desegregation; the other two guests were Attorney General Robert Kennedy and longtime NAACP leader Roy Wilkins.

The University of Georgia had been integrated before Sanders took office. The sprawling Atlanta public school system had been desegregated with only minor disturbances. The first black legislator in Georgia since Reconstruction times, Senator Leroy

Johnson, had been elected, and others were certain to follow.

There had been talk in 1963 that President Kennedy was considering dumping Lyndon Johnson as his vice presidential running mate in the 1964 election and turning to another Southerner, possibly Carl Sanders, who seemed to be more closely attuned to the goals of the New Frontier than was the old warhorse from Texas.

Whether Kennedy seriously entertained such a plan will never be known. An assassin's bullet in Dallas on November 22, 1963, put Lyndon Baines Johnson in the White House.

So in the summer of 1964, Sanders was busy compiling an enviable record as governor of his state and considering running for the United States Senate, a course he later abandoned.

Then on the quiet morning of July 11, 1964, Sanders's carefully nurtured image of a newly progressive Georgia was shattered. Nightriders murdered a black United States Army Reserve officer on a backroad in northeast Georgia.

The first word to the governor came from Major Barney Ragsdale, director of the Georgia Bureau of Investigation, who was contacted by Sheriff Dewey Seagraves of Madison County, where the killing of Lemuel Penn had occurred.

Before Sanders could assess the magnitude of the crime, President Johnson was on the phone to him. The president had been informed, by Secretary of Defense Robert MacNamara, of the killing of Colonel Penn, who had been traveling on U.S. Army orders. Washington had quickly been notified by the Fort Benning authorities. Johnson said he was directing the FBI to move in force into the case. Sanders responded that he already had ordered the Georgia Bureau of Investigation to launch a full-scale investigation of the killing. No matter, said Johnson, J. Edgar Hoover had already been notified.

FBI director Hoover was aboard a plane when he learned by radio of the Penn killing. "If they get away with this, they'll think they can get away with anything," Hoover told his assistant Clyde Tolson. "Ask Atlanta how many extra agents they need. I want them all to report there today." By nightfall, seventy-eight FBI agents were combing the northeast Georgia countryside for clues. As it turned out, a call from Joe Ponder, special agent in charge of the Atlanta FBI office, to FBI agent Robert Kane in Scranton, Pennsylvania, at 3:30 on July 11, provided the investigators with the names of the prime suspects.

Sanders called an extraordinary Saturday press conference to declare that he was "ashamed for myself and the responsible citizens of Georgia that this occurrence took place in our state.

"What is happening is that we are permitting the rabble-rousers and extremists to become more and more vocal and influential while the good people — the vast majority — are either not concerned enough or not speaking out as they should," Sanders declared.

"If we want to see our state destroyed, our citizens demoralized and the very foundation of our nation undermined, we have only to let this type of individual assume greater prominence and eventually take over, and this will be the end of America."

5 • Return of the Klan

THE PATTERN of Klan violence that would in July of 1964 lead to the random murder of an innocent man on his way home from army training was visible in Athens and even on the University of Georgia campus in the winter of 1961.

The Klan had had ample time and encouragement to organize forces in the years after the landmark decision of the United States Supreme Court in 1954 ordering the desegregation of public schools over the nation.

The decision declared segregated schools inherently unequal. To the amazement perhaps of the Supreme Court justices and certainly of the attorneys who won the case, there was little immediate reaction. Some Southern political figures had mildly encouraging things to say about how the decision would be implemented peacefully. Others were noncommittal. That passive phase passed quickly, however. Within little more than one year, virtually every political figure in the South was denouncing the Supreme Court decision and openly talking of ways to prevent its implementation.

No leadership on the issue came from the White House. President Dwight D. Eisenhower refused publicly to say that he approved of the school integration decision in what was either the most colossally callous or the most morally obtuse action of his presidency. Ike paid a price. His failure to offer any moral leadership encouraged those who wanted to maintain segregated schools; in the end, it was Eisenhower who was forced to send United States troops to Little Rock, Arkansas, to put down open defiance of the federal government and of the school desegregation decision.

The University of Georgia in Athens was integrated by federal court order in January 1961. But integration was not accepted at first. Court order or no, an estimated two thousand students, townspeople and "others" cursed and threw stones and bottles and set fires outside a women's dormitory into which Charlayne Hunter, the university's first black woman student, had just moved.

Gov. Ernest Vandiver ordered Miss Hunter and Hamilton Holmes, the university's first black male student, removed from the college campus until authorities could regain control of the situation. The action was ostensibly for the safety of the two students; many people hoped they would not return to the campus at all. The federal courts swiftly ordered the students admitted to the campus again, and this time they stayed. Both students, incidentally, compiled distinguished records at the University of Georgia and in subsequent careers — Charlayne Hunter as a journalist with *The. New York Times* and in public television, Hamilton Holmes at Emory Medical School and as a doctor in the career footsteps of his physician grandfather.

Vandiver's executive secretary, Peter Zack Geer, commended the mob at the University of Georgia for showing how it felt about court-ordered integration. Geer was to ride that emotional wave to election as lieutenant governor of Georgia one year later.

Vandiver was chagrined. Two years earlier he had run for governor on a segregationist platform, promising "No! Not one!" But after taking office, Vandiver saw the futility of his segregation pledge and attempted to bring integration to his home state as painlessly and peacefully as possible.

Integration still was not welcomed on the University of Georgia campus or in the city of Athens, where restaurants and other public accommodations remained segregated. In the aftermath of the rioting, *The Athens Banner-Herald* in a front-page editorial declared: "Most people in Athens, the university, and Georgia do not want integration, but they do not want their problems settled by lawless rabble or federal intervention, either."

The editorial was critical of state law enforcement authorities who failed to respond immediately to the call for help when the rioting erupted.

Another incident occurred during the rioting that was almost lost in the news of the day.

Eight Atlanta men were arrested on the Georgia campus on charges of disorderly conduct and carrying a deadly weapon to a public gathering. Athens police found in their car a .45-caliber pistol, two .22 pistols, three .38s, all loaded, and two belts of ammunition. All eight men were identified as members of the Ku Klux Klan.

6 • The Pattern of Violence

FATHER JOHN MULROY was in college in New York when he decided to be a priest, but he did not want to stay in the city. That was not his idea of priesthood. So, as he put it later, he looked around and noticed that there were fewer priests in the state of Georgia "than almost any other place in the civilized world;" only twenty-six were permanently based there. He decided to come to Georgia.

In Athens in the early 1960s, he had some reason to feel that he had done well for a young Catholic priest from Brooklyn trying to make good in the Deep South. He had been able to buy a seventy-six-acre tract of land with an old farmhouse five miles outside the town for a measly $4,800. The archbishop in Atlanta had not fully approved of the purchase, but after all, what could anyone say against such a bargain?

The house and land were to be used by the Roman Catholic church as a camp for underprivileged children, and in Athens in the 1960s most of the campers would have been black. Father Mulroy had the old farmhouse renovated and painted, planned nature trails, and noted with relish that there was a lake where the children could swim.

This was in 1962. The day before the children's camp was to open, the house burned to the ground. Investigators found kerosene-soaked rags everywhere at the scene. The destruction was plainly the work of arsonists.

"We just didn't realize at the time that some people didn't like black people in that section of the county," Father Mulroy recalled later.

Father Mulroy had been assigned to Athens in part as a troubleshooter to help keep the town's Catholic hospital open and work out its problems. He was pastor for eight counties, including Clarke County, and the city of Athens. It was a rather large parish geographically, but Mulroy estimated that only about one-half of one per cent of the people in the eight counties were Roman Catholic. There was the church downtown in Athens, a grade school that had been started by some nuns from Germany, a student center on the university campus, and the St. Mary's Hospital built by two doctors.

Father Mulroy's tenure in Athens in the early and mid-1960s coincided with the time of civil rights controversy and Klan intimidation. The young priest soon discovered the burning of the old farmhouse was only the beginning of racially connected incidents.

There was a number of black workers at the Catholic hospital. The nuns who taught at the parochial school lived on the hospital grounds and they got to know the employees. They soon learned that many of the black workers' children rarely attended Sunday School at any church. The nuns invited them to come by on Saturday mornings to hear Bible stories.

The stories were popular, and the number of children grew to a point that the nuns no longer had room enough in their own quarters. The grade school was available on Saturdays, so the sisters began allowing the children to come down to the school on Saturday mornings to see Bible pictures and other illustrations that fitted into the storytelling.

The public schools in Athens would not be fully integrated for years to come, and this apparent integration of the Catholic parochial school on Prince Avenue, four blocks from the Athens central business district, did not sit well with some local citizens.

The nuns noted that the number of children coming dropped sharply on one particular Saturday. The next Saturday only five children were present. The black youngsters were being intimidated. Cars had started to follow the children as they walked home from the school, driving right up to them and slamming on brakes at the last moment to avoid hitting them. "Keep your black asses out of white churches," was the typical shouted insult.

Nor was that the only effort at instilling fear into children and adults alike.

Father Mulroy lived in the Catholic school building when he first moved to Athens. There was an old home nearby, once the home of General Thomas Carr. The church bought the home and Father Mulroy moved in, living in three renovated rooms.

Black and white children often romped and played together on the front lawn of the old house, an activity that left some white citizens incensed at what they regarded as Father Mulroy's public exhibition of racial integration.

Then the Ku Klux Klan moved the headquarters of its Athens unit (Clarke County Klavern No. 244) into the top floor of an old two-story gas station building directly across the street.

These were supposed to be the new and "different" kind of Klansmen, members of the United Klans of America, Knights of the Ku Klux Klan. Their leader in Georgia was Calvin Craig of Atlanta, the grand dragon, who often showed up at KKK rallies in a business suit. He talked of using political pressures instead of violence. He waged public relations campaigns on behalf of the Klan. But the Athens Klansmen either didn't get the message or didn't know that it took more than votes and talk to keep the "niggers in their place." Clarke County Klavern No. 244 believed in militancy.

Mulroy normally drove back and forth to the hospital at least twice a day, and he began to observe the "characters," as he called them, gathering at the new KKK headquarters. Some looked as if they came from the country, many were unshaven, some wore holsters with two guns in broad daylight.

When the black and white youngsters played together on the big lawn next to Mulroy's home, Klansmen across the way stared in their direction while wearing their loaded pistols and sometimes holding sawed-off shotguns. They seldom spoke, but their message seemed clear.

"I remember the Sunday I finally decided to lay the cards on the table to my congregation," Mulroy said later. "I told them I felt I was in Dodge City before Matt Dillon arrived. I gave an order that no children were to play on the front lawn.

"Some members of my congregation did not understand what I meant about Dodge City and Matt Dillon. They thought I was concerned about the grass on the front lawn and wanted the children to play elsewhere. They did not quite realize that the armed Klansmen across the way seemed capable of hurting children and adults alike."

It was the end of winter and the beginning of spring in 1964.

Some black children who attended the Catholic church lived in a neighborhood right behind The Varsity, a popular Athens drive-in restaurant. They wanted to buy Cokes there, and they could not. They wanted to buy hotdogs, and they could not. They had the money, but they also had black skins, and The Varsity was as segregated as other eating places throughout the South in 1964. One day four of the youngsters came to Father Mulroy and said, "Father, it ain't right," and wanted to know if he would do something about it.

Mulroy told them that he was not sure what he could do about it personally, that in fact The Varsity would serve him because of his white skin. "Why don't you protest?" he said.

The youngsters did. They joined forces with a youth group connected with the local chapter of the NAACP and began mass picketing of The Varsity.

Father Mulroy did not join the picket line, but he worried about the young people who did. One of his white parishioners ran the Dairy Queen next door to The Varsity, and Mulroy would go there at night to stand and watch the young picketers, just to be sure they were safe. Another observer who remained discreetly on the sidelines was Robert Kane, the local FBI agent. He had no jurisdiction in any conflicts involving the young picketers, but he had a hunch that serious trouble was brewing as a result of their activities. He was right.

One day the picketers asked Father Mulroy if they could borrow the processional cross, a crucifix with a figure of Jesus on it. He agreed. The night Father Mulroy remembered best of those long vigils was the first time he saw the young people marching in a single line, the first youngster holding the crucifix, the others holding signs quoting Bible verses. "I was hungry," read one sign followed by another, "And you would not give me anything to eat." And other signs: "I was thirsty. And you did not give me a drink. As long as you have done it to me." Mulroy was deeply moved. The Bible verses on the signs meant to him that the young people had understood the things they talked about in church.

"The whole thing," he remembered later, "so infuriated the Klan, who are supposed to be God-fearing Christian men, that one of the Klan's members ran across Broad Street and pointed at the crucifix in absolute horror and disgust and yelled out at the top of his lungs, 'That's Catholic!' and the little kid who was holding the cross kept marching but answered him saying, 'I know, I is one.' These kids were unbelievable. The adults had never done things like that, you know, and they were very much intimidated. How the kids got the guts, I don't know. They just figured it wasn't right."

The Athens business community tried to ignore the picket line. There was no mention of it in the local newspaper, and a radio station that issued a local printed news sheet each day also failed to take notice of the protests. Even when the Klansmen began coun-terpicketing, the local media did not address the problem, as one businessman put it some years later, ". . . seemingly for the good of the community. We thought the protest would be settled soon. And we thought the Klansmen only represented a handful of troublemakers."

An FBI agent said Clarke County Ku Klux Klan chapter (Klavern No. 244) boasted at the peak of Klan activity that it had on its rolls nearly four hundred active dues-paying members and silent but financially supportive citizens. By the time Lt. Col. Lemuel Penn was slain, the Athens chapter had been pared down to a hardcore membership of twenty-nine that included six who were members of the Athens group's tough "security patrol."

In addition, Athens-area Klansmen openly fraternized with some policemen and even traded firearms with local law officers.

An agent of the Georgia Bureau of Investigation was awarded a pistol by the Klan for his success in recruiting new KKK members.

The young black picketers made sport of the Klan counterpickets, as on the night when the black picketers showed up wearing white sheets to match the Klansmen's robes. It seemed to be such innocent fun. The Klansmen didn't think so. At one point during the picketing, a Klansman struck an elderly bystander with a pistol. There was pushing and shoving. White ministers who drove some of the picketers home at night reported being followed.

The Athens Ministerial Association met with Athens Mayor Julius Bishop and asked his help. He said that the Klansmen were within their rights and that the guns they brandished were not illegal. He promised to take action if there were any overt acts of violence.

The Klan's activities spread from the Varsity controversy. There were reports of young black couples being stopped by armed Klansmen and questioned about their destinations. Guns were fired into the air and into the ground at the feet of frightened blacks.

That was just the beginning of the kind of terror that leads inevitably to maiming and murder. Consider some of the other incidents:

—In the spring of 1964, James "Preacher" Potts was a helper in Herbert Guest's busy automobile repair shop in Athens. He was known as Guest's black "gofer."

Shortly before midnight on March 7, 1964, Guest sent Preacher Potts on what Potts thought was one of those "gofer" errands. He sent him to repair a stalled car at the rear of the Moina Michael Auditorium beyond the Athens city limits on the highway to Atlanta. More than two years later, on the witness stand in a federal district court, Potts recalled the chilling occurrence at the auditorium:

"I noticed the place was dark. . . I went around back. Just as I cut the lights off, about eighteen hooded Klansmen came out. . . One of them pulled the key out of the ignition. One said, 'Jimmy, what have you been doing with your money?' I said, 'I don't have any money.' He said, 'Oh yes, you have,' and he said, 'Bend over that hood.' "

Potts said he bent across the hood of the automobile and the Klansmen gave him eighteen lashes across the buttocks with a leather strap.

When he was released, Potts said he returned in pain to Guest's garage, but did not tell Herbert Guest what had happened. He did not have to. Guest ordered him to sit down and jokingly asked if Potts wanted a pillow. Later Potts said he received a phone call. The voice was the same as that of the hooded Klansman who did all the talking at the auditorium.

"Preacher, you got off light that time. You might not be so lucky the next time," the caller warned.

Potts identified the caller and the nightriders' spokesman as Joseph Howard Sims. He said he knew him by his voice and the eyes he could see through the slits in the hood.

—On June 21, a shotgun was discharged into the rear door of apartment number three of the Broad Acres Apartments in Athens. Two of the pellets struck John Clink, age nineteen, black, in the face near the right eye. Two other pellets struck Alice Farr, thirteen, also black.

Investigators established that the shotgun blast was discharged from one of the two cars at the scene. The cars were owned by members of Clarke County Klavern No. 244.

John Clink was permanently blinded in one eye. Herbert Guest, the Athens garage operator, was subsequently arrested, along with other Klansmen, and convicted and fined for discharging firearms within the city.

—July 4, 1964, may have been a holiday for most people, but not for the leaders of Clarke County Klavern No. 244. Holiday or not, they buckled on their pistols and went looking for trouble.

Athens policeman Carleton Farr was standing on a main thoroughfare in Athens when a car with a New Jersey license plate pulled up. It was occupied by an elderly black couple. The man asked Officer Farr for directions to Atlanta.

While the officer was giving directions, Joseph Howard Sims walked up, poked his head into the window of the car and said, "Get your black asses back up North where you came from."

"Evidently, it must've scared them because they dug off," Officer Farr later testified in court. Did the policeman arrest Sims and his sidekick, identified as Cecil William Myers? No. After all, as Officer Farr explained, Sims apologized to him for cursing the black couple.

Officer Farr testified that he saw no weapons at the time. But his partner, Officer Gerald M. Flanagan, testified that both Sims and Myers were wearing pistols when Sims confronted the out-of-state black couple.

Later that night, while on patrol, Officer Flanagan said he saw Sims and Myers at a drive-in restaurant frequented by blacks. Both were still wearing their guns.

—Frank Gilmore noticed a station wagon following him home. After he went into his house, he later testified in federal court, there was a rap at the door. When Gilmore opened the door, he said, several white men carrying guns asked him his name and address and then left.

Shortly afterwards, according to Gilmore's testimony, the Athens police came, arrested Gilmore and held him in jail overnight.

Gilmore had been arrested on a charge of "investigation," Athens police records show, on a complaint by Joseph Howard Sims and James S. Lackey. Lackey said he had spotted a prowler around his home.

The Athens, Georgia, police in 1964 may have had their hands full, trying to contain KKK nightriding activities and watching over black demonstrators demanding equal treatment at public accommodations, but they were still an obliging lot. An Athens policeman testified in federal court that when Joseph Howard Sims asked him for identification on a license plate of a car occupied by a black man, the officer gave the Klansman the man's name and address.

These were only a few of the incidents of violence and intimidation that occurred in the months and weeks preceding the murder of Lemuel Penn. They were carefully documented in public trials that grew out of the killing of Colonel Penn. Investigators estimate that the hardcore group of KKK nightriders was on the prowl an average of three nights a week beginning in the late winter of 1964.

Incidentally, Father Mulroy and the members of his church pushed on with their plans for a summer camp for disadvantaged youngsters despite the burning of the farmhouse and disruption of their initial plans. They built a swimming pool and put up some new buildings — tin buildings on concrete slabs. The buildings were hot inside in the summer, but they were also safe from the kerosene rags of the nightriders.

Lemuel Penn

Georgia Penn

Deputy Sherriff H.L. Pulleam points to the bullet holes in the window of the car that Lemuel Penn was driving.

Linda, 13, Sharon, 10, and Lemuel Jr., 5, the children of Lemuel A. Penn, pose in front of their home.

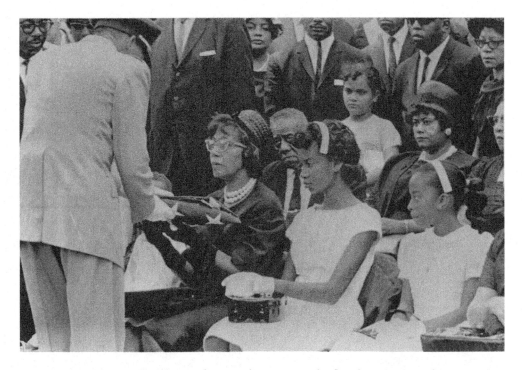

Linda and Sharon Penn look on as their mother receives the flag that was draped over her husband's coffin from Lt. Col. James A. Connett, chaplain at Ft. Myers, Va. Penn was buried at Arlington National Cemetery with full military honors on July 14, 1964.

Cecil Myers (foreground) and Howard Sims (right), two of the men acquitted of Lemuel's Penn's murder, are restrained after an SCLC photographer (far left) ignored their request not to take their picture, October 13, 1965.

7 • Code Name: Penvic

ON THE morning of July 11, 1964, as Madison County Sheriff Dewey Seagraves notified Georgia authorities of the Penn slaying, Joseph J. Casper, assistant director of the Federal Bureau of Investigation, was relaxing on annual leave at Myrtle Beach, South Carolina, where he would retire a few years later.

Robert Kane, resident agent of the FBI in Athens, was vacationing with his family in Pennsylvania. Kane would offer a prophetic suggestion for handling the investigation when contacted only hours after Penn's death.

Special agent Jack B. Simpson reported to work in Atlanta to catch up on a backlog of work relating to routine cases, as did Joseph K. Ponder, special agent in charge of the Atlanta FBI office, and his assistant, Eugene Stewart.

Shortly before 10:00 A.M., the Augusta FBI office was notified by the Criminal Investigation Division of the Army Military Police Corps of Penn's death. Augusta FBI phoned Atlanta FBI at 10:15 A.M. Ponder immediately dispatched agents to the scene. He placed his assistant, Eugene Stewart, in charge of the investigation. Jack Simpson also was sent to Athens.

Meanwhile, in Washington, Walter W. Jenkins, special assis-

33

tant to President Johnson, asked for a full report on the slaying of
Penn as soon as possible. He said the president wanted the FBI to
give "top priority" to the Penn case.

FBI director Hoover focused full attention on the investigation.
In addition to ordering large numbers of investigators to the scene,
he sent the best technical assistance and clerical help to Athens to
aid in the massive search for Lemuel Penn's killer. The director also
decided the case needed a code name. He called it Penvic — a
contraction of Penn and Victim. As soon as FBI agents established
that Penn was not the victim of some "hanky-panky back at Benning," Hoover wired Joe Ponder:

"Adoption of the word 'Penvic' has been approved as the caption
for this case for use in intra-bureau communications only. It is not
to be used in investigative reports or letterhead memoranda prepared for dissemination. Advise auxiliary offices."

By 1:15 P.M. Atlanta SAC (special agent in charge) Ponder had
given Hoover's office a complete rundown on the killing.

Shortly after Ponder phoned Hoover's office, John Doar, chief for
the Civil Rights Division of the Department of Justice, phoned
Alex Rosen, one of Hoover's top assistants. The bureau was not
especially happy to hear from Doar, who also happened to be a
confidant of Attorney General Robert Kennedy.

In a memorandum written that day and made available in 1979
by the FBI under provisions of the Freedom of Information Act,
Hoover's assistant Rosen wrote:

"Doar stated he had been talking to Secretary of Defense
McNamara and that he desired to let the Bureau know that the
Department of Defense had a number of investigators who were
available for the use of the FBI in connection with this investigation. Doar asked how many agents we had at the scene. He was
advised there were a number of agents at the scene and others were
en route at the time.

"Doar stated he knew the Bureau was conducting an all-out
investigation, but he desired to furnish a couple of investigators
which we might consider for what they were worth in connection
with our investigation. He thought it would be appropriate to
check whether or not the individuals had endeavored to use the
facilities of any restaurant, service station, etc., in connection

with their travel. In this connection, Doar was thinking [of] the possibility that the incident may have been occasioned by these individuals using a restaurant or other accommodation to the resentment of some of the white individuals in the area."

If Doar believed that Penn was slain because he had violated some segregationist tradition of the South, he was wrong.

Another Hoover assistant, Courtney Evans, interrupted assistant director Joseph Casper's leave at Myrtle Beach and ordered him to Athens to take charge of the investigation. Casper was familiar with Georgia. He had been special agent in charge of the Atlanta office in the 1950s. He later handled some of the bureau's most celebrated cases, including the Frank Sinatra, Jr., kidnapping. The Penn case would prove to be his biggest ever.

Joe Ponder interrupted agent Bob Kane's sojourn in Scranton, Pennsylvania. He ordered Kane back to Georgia. He asked Kane who he thought might have been involved in the killing, and Kane suggested that the investigation focus on Joseph Howard Sims, Herbert Guest, James Lackey, and Denver Phillips. It was 3:30 P.M., less than twelve hours after the killing.

Kane's suggestion on how to channel the investigation was on target, focusing on the KKK and even on the very Klansmen who would later become prime suspects. Kane had been based in Athens for the FBI for eleven years; he had been graduated from the University of Georgia in addition to his normal work. He was, in fact, the single member of the small army of FBI agents working the case who from the beginning had a direct intimate knowledge of the Athens community.

The Klan was not unaware of the threat posed by Kane in the aftermath of the Penn killing. Whenever there was trouble involving the Klan in the Athens area, Kane always seemed to show up, never to make an arrest but always to ask a few questions and take a few notes. The hardcore leaders of the KKK also were certain, although they couldn't prove it, that several of their members were paid informers who reported to Kane regularly about KKK activities.

During the tumultuous spring and summer of 1964, Kane's life was threatened openly by a member of the Klan security patrol. His family was harassed by crank callers. His wife slept with a shotgun under her bed when Kane was out trying to keep tabs on the dusk-to-dawn riding members of the local klavern.

The investigation of the Penn slaying continued four weeks without an arrest. There were reports that one of Penn's companions was a big winner in a poker game shortly before they left Fort Benning. That had to be checked out. It was untrue.

There were dozens of leads that came to dead ends, anonymous telephone calls that could not be traced. Every scrap of information, false or true, significant or insignificant, was recorded and ultimately passed along to Hoover's office.

On July 13, Hoover's aide Rosen was informed by memorandum:

"At 12:42 A.M., Assistant Director Joseph Casper, Athens, Georgia, telephonically advised that the night security clerk of the Atlanta, Georgia, office had received a telephone call from an unknown white male who stated, 'You know who got this nigger up at Athens. We're going to get another one tonight.' The caller then hung up.

"Assistant Director Casper stated that the local police department and Georgia Bureau of Investigation had been advised. Attempts to locate the sheriff had been negative; however, the sheriff would be advised as soon as he could be contacted.

"Five patrols of Agents are patrolling the area of prior incidents. Assistant Director Casper stated he would keep the Bureau promptly advised of pertinent developments."

The newspapers said the FBI had no leads in the Penn case.

Two days after the investigation began, Madison County Sheriff Dewey Seagraves told reporters the FBI was hindering his attempts to track down the killers. Seagraves said local residents were afraid to talk because of the presence of federal agents.

On July 14, FBI agents scurried to Madison County after two white teenagers reported their windshield was shattered by a bullet fired from a station wagon occupied by four blacks. After extensive investigation, agents determined that the windshield had been struck by "a thrown object, probably a rock." The marauding station wagon also was found. It was occupied by "unarmed white kids," investigators reported.

The Klan had its own version of why Penn had been killed. A few days after the slaying, an FBI informant attended an initiation ceremony in the Athens klavern of the United Klans of America. The informant's account, released in 1979 under provisions of the Freedom of Information Act, follows:

"All of the men from Athens were armed with sidearms with the exception of [two names]. These men have 'pistol toters' permits and most of them carry .38 caliber Smith and Wesson revolvers. Inside the Klavern, hanging on the wall are several rifles, the majority of these being British made 303 rifles. There are 4 or 5 persons in the Athens Klavern that have double-barreled sawed-off shotguns but these weapons have reportedly been checked out to insure they are the proper length not to violate any law. No shotguns were observed inside the klavern.

"Several klansmen present mentioned that PENN had a run-in with someone back at the base (Ft. Benning), and this person was merely getting even with PENN. This version of the killing was just general talk.

"The general trend of thought of klansmen in Athens was that someone other than a klansman was responsible for the shooting and that in all probability was another Negro.

"Their feeling toward the death of PENN is that it is just one less Negro and 'good' for whoever did it.

"Several klansmen made the statement that they would give a month's pay if it could be shown that a Negro was responsible for the shooting and he could be caught and convicted for it in order that this could be given newspaper publicity.

"The klansmen appear to have no plan of action and are just sitting back waiting to see what happens. They feel that it is very humorous, the amount of activity on the part of the FBI in this investigation. . . ."

An FBI agent concluded the account:

"Informant advised that if these klansmen have any knowledge as to the identity of the person responsible for the shooting of PENN, they are very good actors because they appear to know nothing concerning the person or persons responsible.

"These klansmen advised that when they observe someone following them, they go on a wild ride around town and then go home. The Athens Klavern has their own security patrol set up. . .

"Informant advised he did not believe any of the klansmen

would help the GBI [Georgia Bureau of Investigation], or Chief of Police [E.E. Hardy] at Athens, Georgia. He stated they would come nearer to assisting a local police officer. He stated they seemed to direct their criticism of the FBI to the Department of Justice rather than to any actions of individual agents."

On July 17, *The Atlanta Constitution* reported it had been informed by "a reliable source" that a significant lead had been uncovered in connection with Penn's death. Sheriff Seagraves scoffed at the report. The FBI refused to comment.

On July 18, *The Atlanta Constitution* reported that a white man "previously convicted in connection with a shooting involving Negroes" had been questioned by the FBI. Again, the bureau refused to confirm or deny.

Meanwhile, word spread that another black man had been murdered in the area before Penn was killed. Investigators exhumed the body of a forty-nine-year-old black man found dead July 6 in Madison County a few miles from where Penn was killed. Dr. Larry Howard of the State Crime Laboratory examined the body of Benny Johnson, alias Bliss Swift. Dr. Howard determined that Johnson died of injuries suffered when he was struck by a train. There was no connection between the death of "Bliss Swift" and Lemuel Penn.

Paperwork in the makeshift FBI operational headquarters at the Key to America Motel in Athens continued to grow. Special agent Edward Kassinger was put in charge of writing and coordinating reports. He worked more than twelve hours a day every day. Still, he couldn't keep up.

Casper informed Hoover's office that five members of the Clarke County Klavern had participated in racial violence recently and "are known to have purchased five double-barreled shotguns recently."

Hoover responded by teletype: "YOU ARE INSTRUCTED TO IMMEDIATELY, IF NOT ALREADY DONE, THOROUGHLY RUN OUT THE PURCHASE OF SHOTGUNS. CONTINUE TO SUBMIT SUMMARY TELETYPE OF NATURE, SCOPE AND DETAILS OF INVESTIGATION BEFORE TWELVE MIDNIGHT EACH DAY. INCLUDE DETAILS RE INVESTIGATION IN YOUR TELETYPE OF THIS DATE [July 13]."

Despite the numerous wild-goose chases and blind alleys the investigators found themselves in, the main thrust of the FBI's investigation quickly focused on the Ku Klux Klan. The day after the murder, FBI agent Kane, along with Athens Police Chief E.E. Hardy, interviewed Thomas B. Whitehead of Athens, exalted cyclops of Clarke County Klavern No. 244, United Klans of America, Knights of the Ku Klux Klan. Chief Hardy was one of the few local officers trusted by the FBI. He also was the only local lawman who was determined to halt the Klan-instigated violence that plagued Athens that summer. (Chief Hardy was praised repeatedly for his work in memoranda released by the FBI in 1979 in connection with the Penn case.)

In a teletype message to Hoover from the Atlanta FBI office shortly before midnight on July 12, Atlanta gave this account of the interview of Whitehead and other Klan members by Kane and Chief Hardy:

"[Whitehead] STATED THAT HE HAS NO KNOWLEDGE CONCERNING THE SHOOTING OF LT. COL. LEMUEL A. PENN....OTHER THAN WHAT HE HAD READ IN THE NEWSPAPERS.

"WHITEHEAD ADVISED THAT HE DID NOT THINK ANY MEMBER OF THE ATHENS KLAVERN OF THE KKK WERE INVOLVED IN THE SHOOTING. HE STATED THAT HE DEPLORES VIOLENCE AND HAS CAUTIONED MEMBERS OF HIS KLAVERN NOT TO USE VIOLENCE. HE ALSO STATED THAT HE HAD TWO OR THREE MEMBERS, NAMES WHICH HE DID NOT FURNISH, THAT HE COULD NOT CONTROL THEIR ACTIONS. HE SAID THAT IF HE HEARD ANYTHING WHICH WOULD BE OF ASSISTANCE, THAT HE WOULD CONTACT THIS OFFICE.

"[Name deleted by the FBI Freedom of Information Section] ADVISED HE RECENTLY BECAME AN INACTIVE MEMBER OF THE (KLAN). HE STATED THAT HIS REASON FOR BECOMING INACTIVE WAS THE INCREASED VIOLENT METHODS BEING USED BY KLANSMEN HERBERT GUEST, HOWARD SIMS, CECIL MYERS, JAMES LACKEY, AND (FNU) FOLENDORE.

"[Name Deleted] ADVISED THAT HE HAD NO INFOR-
MATION CONCERNING THE SHOOTING OF LT. COL.
LEMUEL A. PENN ON THE MORNING OF JULY 11 LAST,
OTHER THAN WHAT HE HAS READ IN THE NEWSPA-
PERS.

"[Name Deleted] STATED THAT GUEST, SIMS, AND
MYERS HAVE HURT THE KLAN IN ATHENS BY HAVING
BEEN INVOLVED IN VIOLENCE. HE ADVISED THAT HE
WILL MAKE AN EFFORT TO OBTAIN INFORMATION
CONCERNING THE SHOOTING AND WILL ADVISE THIS
OFFICE.

"INDEPENDENT INVESTIGATION, SECURITY PATROL,
LOCAL CHAPTER, UNITED KLANS OF AMERICA,
ATHENS, GA.

"THESE INDIVIDUALS PLACED IN DOWNTOWN
ATHENS AREA APPROXIMATELY ONE THIRTY AM, JULY
ELEVEN LAST.

JOSEPH HOWARD SIMS, WHITE MALE, DOB [date of
birth] FOUR TWENTY-SEVEN, TWENTY-THREE, CLARKE
COUNTY, GA.

HERBERT GUEST, WHITE MALE, DOB JULY THIRTY-
ONE, TWENTY-SEVEN, ELBERT COUNTY, GA.

JAMES LACKEY, WHITE MALE, AGE APPROXIMATELY
TWENTY-FIVE.

DENVER WILLIS PHILLIPS, WHITE MALE, DOB JULY
TWENTY-ONE NINETEEN FORTY, MADISON COUNTY,
GA.

BUREAU SEE ATLANTA TEL DATED JUNE TWENTY-
ONE, NINETEEN SIXTY FOUR, CAPTIONED HERBERT
GUEST, ET AL, RACIAL MATTERS, ATHENS, GA."

Even if Athens officials ignored the earlier violence of the KKK,
the FBI and the Department of Justice did not. Now they had also
placed the prime suspects in downtown Athens early on the
morning of July 11.

The teletype message continued:

THIS TEL [dated June 21, 1964] RELATED TO ARREST BY
ATHENS, GA., PD, OF HERBERT GUEST CHARGED WITH
DISCHARGING FIREARMS IN CITY. DISPOSITION FINED

ONE HUNDRED FIVE DOLLARS OR ONE HUNDRED
DAYS.

PAUL STRICKLAND ALSO CHARGED DISCHARGING
FIREARMS AS HE AND GUEST WERE IDENTIFIED AS
BEING IN A CAR WHEN SHOTS WERE FIRED INTO THE
AIR IN FRONT OF A NEGRO APARTMENT BUILDING.
STRICKLAND FINED ONE HUNDRED FIVE DOLLARS OR
ONE HUNDRED DAYS.

THIRTY MINUTES LATER PAUL STRICKLAND AND
DENVER PHILLIPS WERE IDENTIFIED AS BEING IN THE
CAR FROM WHICH A SHOTGUN WAS FIRED INTO THE
BACK DOOR OF A NEGRO APARTMENT.

INFO DEVELOPED DURING CURRENT INVESTIGA-
TION, ATHENS, RESULTED IN IDENTIFICATION OF
SIMS, GUEST, PHILLIPS ALONG WITH AN INDIVIDUAL
KNOWN ONLY TO DATE AS JAMES LACKEY, AS HAVING
BEEN TOGETHER APPROXIMATELY ONE THIRTY A.M.,
JULY ELEVEN LAST, IN THE DOWNTOWN ATHENS
AREA, WEARING SIDEARMS.

IN VIEW OF THIS AND CIRCUMSTANCES LEADING
TO PRIOR ARRESTS BY ATHENS PD, THIS PHASE BEING
PURSUED VIGOROUSLY.

8 • Prescription for Guilt

ONE OF THE FEW elected public officials in Athens that summer who offered active help to the FBI in its investigation of the Penn case was Superior Court Judge James Barrow. He made a special trip to the Athens Post Office building where the FBI was headquartered to talk to the man in charge, FBI Assistant Director Joseph Casper, and volunteer any help he could give. Judge Barrow's views on the Klan were known and had already subjected him to criticism from some of his fellow townspeople, people who said he had "overreacted" to the Klan demonstrations and violence.

That was not the judge's feeling. He was deeply disturbed by the lack of strong law enforcement and prosecution in connection with Klan activities.

The judge contacted Casper on the night of July 15 and told him that he had conferred with the solicitor general (district attorney) of Clarke County concerning the status of the investigation. Barrow agreed with the prosecutor that there did not yet seem to be the kind of evidence that warranted prosecution, but, as the Athens investigation team informed Hoover's office in a teletype, the judge seemed "well aware of local activities of rabid segregationists."

The judge had more to say. If the investigation could turn up enough information to lead to the successful prosecution of the case, he would convene a grand jury as swiftly as possible. The earliest scheduled date would be just over two weeks away, during the first week of August. The judge added that he would "build a fire under the prosecution" if there seemed to be sufficient evidence.

Judge Barrow would later send one of the Penn murder suspects to prison for an equally violent but totally unrelated crime.

Meanwhile, the FBI began receiving tips from other sources — paid informants within the Klan, local law enforcement agencies, and a few concerned citizens. Clarke County Sheriff Tommy Huff provided the bureau with a list of possible suspects. All the tips and lists had a common thread: the same names that FBI agent Kane had given his boss, Joe Ponder, less than twelve hours after Penn's death.

The federal investigation moved in earnest now, and Casper's team zeroed in on a half dozen suspects in the Klan, among them:

Joseph Howard Sims, age forty-five, medium height, hefty; a skilled machinist, father of eight, navy veteran of World War II. He was the Clarke County Klavern Kladd (sergeant-at-arms). Sims had served the Klan in demonstrations in St. Augustine, Florida, and Birmingham, Alabama, in addition to carrying out acts of violence and intimidation in Athens. He was an avid gun collector and racing-car buff. Known for his quick temper, Sims complained often of severe migraine headaches.

Herbert Guest, age thirty-six, a 282-pound garage operator with a first-grade education. He kept shotguns and rifles hanging on the walls of his garage. Black-haired, with several front teeth missing, Guest frequently complained about his health. His wife, Blanche, dominated the Guest household.

Cecil William Myers, age twenty-five, tall, slender, dark crew cut, wore glasses, father of three, yarn picker in a textile mill. He was proud to be a Klansman and wore a pistol strapped to his hip to prove it.

Then there was James S. Lackey, age twenty-five. His name kept turning up in connection with the investigation. But the FBI couldn't figure at first exactly where Lackey fit in.

James S. Lackey was the night manager of People's Oil Company in Athens. That meant he was the sole gas-pumper at night at a small discount-gas service station. His pay was low, and he did not especially like the job. He lived with his wife and children in a small house in East Athens, an area that today would be called "transitional" because of its mixture of black and white residents. Yet East Athens had been "transitional" for years. It is where poor people of both races often found themselves living side by side.

Lackey had psychological problems, court testimony later indicated. His head was large and slightly misshapen. He felt that people stared at him and made fun of him. He also felt that he was not very bright, and that somehow his misshapen head was the reason for his low IQ.

He was concerned about leaving his wife and children alone at night. He expressed that worry to an Athens policeman who advised Lackey to join the Ku Klux Klan for "protection."

Lackey said later that he paid five dollars and became a member of the United Klans of America, Knights of the Ku Klux Klan. "For the first time in my life, I belonged to something," he later told his attorneys.

He found in the Klan just what he was looking for — protection, companionship, friendship. While Lackey worked, the wives of other Klansmen would visit his wife and stay with her, sometimes all night. After he finished work, Lackey started riding around town with the armed Klansmen to "make sure everything was all right."

Special FBI agents Jack Simpson, from the Atlanta office, and Clarence Brom, assigned to the Penn case from Newark, New Jersey, were ordered to find out how — if at all — Lackey fitted into the Penn picture. He became an obsession for both men.

Simpson recalled years later:

"Working on background and observing Lackey's movements took a great deal of time and required one hundred percent concentration. Brom and I listened to information filtered to us by case coordinator Edward Kassinger and special agent James Henderson and from other team members who reported their daily progress through assistant director Casper. My partner and I gradually found that our whole lives began to revolve around our target. We talked about the case before we went to sleep at night. We talked about it while we ate and while we rode around Athens covering our leads. Then at night we attended meetings with other agents and took notes."

After keeping him under surveillance for several days, Simpson and Brom decided it was time to interview James S. Lackey personally.

"We waited until Lackey completed work on July 29, 1964," Simpson recalled. "We dropped by the service station, displayed to him our credentials, and introduced ourselves. We were very careful to 'play it by the book.' We advised Lackey of his constitutional rights, and we let him become aware we were interested in him. We dropped hints about knowing who he was, where he lived, who he associated with, and some of the intimate facts about his personal life. If he did, in fact, have a guilty conscience, we reasoned that a sympathetic approach was proper, and at no time did we use any rough language, tactics, nor did we threaten him.

"We still didn't really know if we were dealing with a potential Klan informant, a possible witness, or a genuine suspect."

Simpson casually mentioned during the course of that interview that the FBI sometimes paid as much as $3,000 for information in an important case such as this one.

Lackey insisted he had no knowledge of the Penn case. In fact, he said, not only was he not near the scene of the killing when it occurred, he knew for a fact that neither were Howard Sims and Cecil Myers. He was prepared to swear to his whereabouts as well as to give his friends, Sims and Myers, a solid alibi. In fact, he would do better than swear. He would submit to a polygraph examination to prove he was telling the truth.

The initial interview with Lackey hardly produced the kind of information Brom and Simpson were seeking. Nevertheless, they parted on good terms with Lackey and promised they would talk to him again.

Other teams of FBI agents were assigned to follow and question other KKK members, certain the Klan was involved in the Penn murder and that persistent effort would produce the needed evidence.

But not all the investigators used orthodox tactics in dealing with their "targets." Agents William Watry and Arthur Hamilton presented a birthday cake to Herbert Guest on July 31, 1964. It was Herbert's thirty-seventh birthday.

"Don't ask me why they gave it to him," Guest's wife told reporters. "Herbert wanted to sit down and eat it. But I wouldn't let him. I told him he didn't know what the FBI might've put in the cake." Mrs. Guest said she wrapped the cake in wax paper and placed it in their home freezer.

The FBI men left the cake at Guest's garage, then later saw the overweight garage operator on an Athens street, told him of the cake, and said, "Happy birthday, Herbert."

The white-frosted coconut cake was decorated with thirty-seven pink and white candles — and one blood-red candle.

"I believe the cake was just their way of letting Herbert know they knew all about him," Tom Stephens, a friend of Guest, said at the time.

The cake would later be presented in federal court as evidence that the FBI harassed Guest. But an agent testified that the bureau only wanted to be "cordial" in dealing with the man who surren-dered five shotguns to the G-men after the Penn killing.

On August 1, Brom and Simpson again picked up Lackey at the People's Oil Company and took him to the Athens federal building for further interrogation. Simpson recalled later, "Before the interview began we again reminded him of his constitutional rights and reminded him that we were not promising him anything or threatening him in any manner in order to get him to give us an interview. On the occasion of the particular contact, Lackey complained of a stomachache and said he was tired, and we im-mediately terminated the interview about 4 P.M. and drove him back to the oil company."

Simpson and Brom felt they were on to something. On August 3, they again tried to question Lackey at his home. He told them he was too ill to talk; they advised him to consult a physician.

On the night of August 5, the agents dropped by the People's Oil Company to check on the state of Lackey's health. He said he felt better and agreed to be questioned again the following day.

Here is Simpson's account of that critical interrogation session:

"On August 6 at 8:55 A.M. we went to Lackey's residence and

picked him up at his invitation. Brom and I began to think that Lackey's sense of decency was getting to him. We both felt that Lackey had some sense of guilt about something and that he wanted to tell us something of importance.

"We began the interview in the usual way, advising Lackey of his constitutional rights. And again we reminded him that no promises were being made, no rewards offered.

"Brom began talking with Lackey in generalities, asking about the state of his health, asking him if he were sure he felt well enough to be interviewed. Lackey said he felt OK.

"I said to him, 'James, we have been doing some checking around, and some of our friends tell us that Sims and Myers can be put on the Athens streets at the right time for the Penn murder. Why would you alibi or try to alibi for them? We think part of the reason you had stomach trouble this past week is nerves. You've got something inside you that you don't want to be there anymore. We now think after having listened to you and having talked with others that you really know something and we believe you really have a lot of good in you and this wants to come out. Why don't you get yourself some relief? Get rid of what worries you. Tell us what it is that's bothering you so much.' "

Lackey dropped his head for a moment, then looked directly at the FBI men. "I'm going to tell you the truth. I drove the car. But I didn't think those sonofabitches were going to kill him," he said matter-of-factly.

Lackey's admission hit the two FBI agents "like a bombshell," Simpson remembered later. It was the breakthrough in an incredible case.

"James Lackey's motive in confessing was not that he had been made promises, but rather was relief from guilt. Basically, Lackey seemed like a decent person who got caught up in something because he wanted to be part of the gang. He wanted companionship and approval from his peers. He was not an habitual criminal, and he was not always seen at The Varsity parading with the Klansmen. He was basically a man who worked hard and took care of his family. His guilt in this particular case tortured him, and he sought personal relief from that torture," said Simpson.

The case began to come together. Simpson informed Casper of

the confession. Other statements were taken from Lackey, adding details and bits and pieces to the puzzle.

Agents Watry and Hamilton picked up Herbert Guest and brought him to the federal building — without shoes. Guest refused to put on shoes, but he gave the agents statements that corroborated much of what Lackey had told Simpson and Brom.

A confession and corroborating statement plus strong physical and circumstantial evidence — it looked airtight.

Guest and Lackey were informed they were under arrest. Federal men arrested Myers and went looking for Sims. They finally found him at Clarke County Klavern No. 244, his favorite haunt. They also seized all of Sims' guns.

In Washington, Attorney General Robert F. Kennedy informed Georgia Penn that the Klansmen had been arrested in connection with her husband's murder.

"People commit crimes like this because they are ignorant. They need education," Mrs. Penn said.

The suspects were charged with federal civil rights violations. Bail was set at $25,000 each. In Madison County, where Penn was slain, Solicitor General Clete Johnson quickly brought murder charges. A grand jury was convened and murder indictments were returned against Sims, Myers and Lackey. Guest was charged as an accessory after the fact, but he was not indicted.

The federal government agreed to step aside and allow the Klansmen to be tried on the more serious state charge of murder. The ends of justice would be realized in the Superior Court of Madison County. Or so the FBI thought.

Years later, agent Jack Simpson remembered Lackey with considerable sympathy. In the trial that would follow, the defense attorneys would allude to Lackey's misshapen head, content that he had a low IQ, and say that he was suspected of being paranoid. But Simpson recalled a different Lackey.

"In all of our contacts with Lackey, neither agent Brom nor I considered Lackey to be an ugly, misshapen person," Simpson said. "We treated him like an individual, and our relationships were cordial and friendly. At no time did we feel that Lackey was anything more than what he was, a working man in the Athens, Georgia, area with a family, a Klansman, a man who needed

friends, and a man with not a great deal of education. Nevertheless, he was a human being with a nice personality and a lot of
goodness in his heart. There may have been some evil there, too,
but in the end most of his goodness showed through."

Simpson had a chance to view the Ku Klux Klan's methods of
operation in that time. He found that the Klansmen considered
themselves patriotic Americans fighting against the enemies of the
people. Those enemies included the FBI, Jews, President Lyndon
Johnson, and anyone else the Klansmen regarded as a threat to the
Southern way of life. "Burnings, shootings, beatings," Simpson
said, "could not then really be regarded as crimes in the eyes of the
Klan; they were, after all, acts of self-defense." Klansmen also had a
strong church orientation and regarded themselves literally as
being against the enemies of Christ in the South.

In thinking on these things, Simpson thought once more with
sympathy about James Lackey.

"I kept wondering, he said, "where did Lackey fit into this
picture? To me he seemed like a young, hardworking fellow with a
sense of family responsibility. He didn't look particularly strong.
He didn't fit into the image of a bully-boy. He wasn't impressive
and he struck me as a follower. He was a man who needed friends.
Was the Klan the only place he could find them?"

On the Saturday before the Penn trial was to begin, Simpson,
along with Solicitor General Clete Johnson and other law enforcement officials, visited Lackey in the Madison County jail.
Lackey assured the investigators that he was in good health and
that he intended to testify for the state. No, he had no misgivings
about his confession. He promised to stick by it to the letter.

9 • Justice in Madison County

MONDAY, AUGUST 31, 1964, was an exciting day for usually sleepy Danielsville, population 363.

The trial of Howard Sims and Cecil Myers for the murder of Lemuel Penn was ready to start in the Madison County seat. The Ladies Auxiliary of the Veterans of Foreign Wars set up a refreshment stand on the courthouse lawn and served Cokes and coffee. Even the defendants seemed in a jovial mood. Both wore short-sleeve shirts and ties and chatted with reporters about their future plans. The pair said they intended to set up an "auto specialty shop" when the trial was over. Sims discussed at length with one reporter the finer points of stock-car racing.

When one writer finally got around to the issue at hand, namely the murder of Lemuel Penn, Sims smiled.

"We're not worried. We know we're going to come out of this all right. We're not guilty."

Sims may not have been worried. But the presiding judge, Carey Skelton, was. In fact, he was fidgety and irritable. A red-faced man in his fifties who had risen to a position of considerable political power in his community, he knew he had suddenly been placed at center stage in a drama of justice that would receive national attention. Carey Skelton wanted the trial to be conducted as properly as possible. Among his first official acts at the opening of the trial, Judge Skelton ordered Sheriff Seagraves to "do something" about the noisy trucks going around the courthouse square in the center of Danielsville.

"I don't exactly know what I can do about that," Sheriff Seagraves responded. Judge Skelton did, however, and he ordered bailiffs in the courtroom to go outside, flag down the trucks, and tell the truckers to "go quietly around the courthouse."

When that didn't work, Judge Skelton called on Georgia State Patrol officers to block off the town square and order each truck to detour entirely around the town of Danielsville.

The judge not only banned cameras and recording equipment from the courtroom, he also prohibited such devices from being placed on the courthouse lawn. Later in the trial, an Associated Press photographer carrying a camera made the mistake of placing one foot on the concrete curb around the small courthouse building. He was immediately arrested for contempt of court. The judge later dismissed the charge. Judge Skelton wanted no bad press for himself or the trial. He invited reporters into his chambers, complained to them of having to preside over such a controversial matter, and asked if there was anything he could do to make their job easier. They asked for more chairs.

The courtroom was packed with at least two hundred and fifty spectators. Approximately forty blacks showed up to witness the proceedings. They were segregated from the whites and peeked down from a tiny balcony overlooking the courtroom.

The families of the defendants took seats directly behind Sims and Myers. Sims's wife and eight children, ages two to sixteen, filled up most of one row of seats. Myers' wife, then in her ninth month of pregnancy, took a seat along with the Myers's three sons, ages two to five.

James Lackey, whose confession would be the centerpiece of the state's case, appeared briefly in the courtroom in the early part of the proceedings. Lackey's wife, his five-year-old daughter, a brother, and both his parents were present.

An impressive array of legal talent lined up on both sides of the case.

Gov. Carl Sanders had personally intervened to appoint Jeff

Wayne, the solicitor general in nearby Hall County, as a special prosecutor. Wayne had been a criminal lawyer for more than twenty years and was regarded by most of his peers as one of the most talented prosecutors in the state. He was joined by the local prosecutor, Clete Johnson, who had a reputation as a competent though plodding trial lawyer. Johnson turned out to be the star orator for the state in the case against Sims and Myers.

Sims and Myers were represented by James Hudson, an ambitious young lawyer from Athens and a Republican candidate for the Georgia House (he later lost the election), and sixty-year-old John Darsey of Commerce, Georgia, a former assistant U.S. attorney general who had prosecuted Japanese Premier Tojo and other ranking Japanese leaders during the war crimes trials after World War II. Lackey was represented by John W. (Billy) Williford, who would soon be a superior court judge from Elberton, Georgia, and young Nicholas Chilivis of Athens, who was destined to become one of the state's most skilled criminal lawyers.

Also present were key witnesses Lt. Col. John D. Howard and Major Charles E. Brown. The prosecution had asked both Brown and Howard to wear army uniforms to try to impress upon the Madison County jurors that they were "men of high caliber, not like the field niggers who lived around Danielsville," as one state attorney explained later.

Howard and Brown arrived at the courthouse in a state patrol vehicle and were immediately escorted to the witness room to await their turn in telling how it was that their traveling companion, Lemuel Penn, came to die.

Ninety-four white persons and two blacks were tapped for petit jury duty that week. It was the first time in anyone's memory that a black person's name had been placed on the Madison County jury list.

Judge Skelton called the court to order exactly fifty-one days after the murder of Lemuel Penn, and jury selection began. The heat was almost stifling inside the tin-roofed courthouse.

Seventy-three prospective jurors were questioned. A panel of twelve white Protestant men was finally seated to decide the fate of Sims and Myers. The two blacks were considered; defense attorney Hudson struck both, without comment.

Meanwhile, Lackey's attorney, Billy Williford, went to Macon Georgia, to file a petition in the U.S. District Court asking that the court intervene and disallow the use of FBI testimony and Lackey's confession.

Lackey was not going to keep his promise after all. He would recant. Even years later, no one could — or would — say why Lackey backed out on the confession. Did he have that old guilt stomachache again? Did someone at the jail remind him that Sims and Myers had befriended him and now he was betraying them?

In the writ in federal court, Lackey alleged that he was arrested by FBI agents on August 6 without being shown a warrant and was told by agents "that his friends had put a noose around his neck and were going to hang him."

Williford's petition contended that Lackey feared statements "had been signed saying he was the guilty party, so he signed another statement."

Lackey's attorney further alleged in federal court that FBI agents arrested Lackey on federal charges when, in fact, no federal crime had been committed, and asserted that this constituted "an arbitrary and unreasonable singling out" of Lackey simply because he was a member of the Ku Klux Klan.

These efforts failed; Federal District Judge William A. Bootle denied Williford's petition. The trial in Danielsville continued.

At the opening of the second day, Judge Skelton summoned one of the defense attorneys, Harold "Hap" Boggs, into his chambers. The judge was worried.

"Hap, I have just learned that the foreman of the jury told someone that he could never vote to convict white men for killing Negroes. When he was examined on *voir dire* yesterday, he said he would be completely impartial. I am going to declare a mistrial."

"Well, your honor, if you do that," Boggs replied, "I'll be obliged to respond."

"What do you mean 'respond'?" Judge Skelton asked uneasily.

"I mean, with the media and all out there, I'll have to call on the court to disqualify itself."

"Why?"

"Well, as I recall, your honor, right after this happened, you told lots of folks you knew nobody around here shot that nigger 'cause, you said, if they were from around here, they'd have killed every nigger in the car, not just one."

Skelton said he would let Boggs know later whether he intended to follow through with his plans to declare a mistrial. It was the last time Boggs and Skelton discussed calling off the trial or disqualifying the court.

(Boggs and Skelton are both dead now. But associates of both men say this was one of Boggs's favorite stories in discussing the defense of the Penn murder suspects.)

The first witness called by the state was Charles E. Brown. Attired in an army dress uniform with three rows of military decorations and a combat infantryman's badge, Brown calmly described the events of July 11. Brown recounted that he was asleep in the right front seat of his car when two shots were fired into it near the Broad River bridge early on the fogbound morning of July 11. "You go to sleep and you wake up to something like that — it is out of this world," Brown testified. "I did not awaken until I heard two reports. I first thought we had blown two tires — bang! bang! I did not know what was going on. I saw Colonel Penn's head slumped on his chest. His hands were not on the steering wheel. I felt something hot on my left arm. It turned out to be blood.

"We've never had trouble with anyone," Brown continued, describing how he and the two other reserve officers left Fort Benning shortly after midnight, then stopped once in Atlanta for gasoline and again in Athens to change drivers.

Brown said that after the shooting, he and Howard removed Penn's body from beneath the wheel and started driving back toward Athens. He said Howard told him a car was following.

"Why did you reverse directions and start back to Athens?" Clete Johnson asked.

"If you had been hit by weapons and were not armed with anything to defend yourself, I don't think you'd continue in the same direction as those lights we saw in the fog," Brown replied.

Defense attorney Hudson came down hard on cross-examination. Brown, who was asleep, could not be absolutely certain that the gunshots which killed Penn "came from outside the car," Hudson shouted. Brown agreed. But it was a futile line of questioning. The next witness, Col. John Howard, swore the shot came from another car. And later in the trial, Dr. Larry Howard of the Georgia State Crime Laboratory would deliver expert testimony that Penn was killed by a shotgun loaded with single-ought buckshot and there was conclusive evidence the shots were fired from another car.

On the stand, Col. Howard corroborated Brown's account of the drive from Fort Benning. Howard said he was awake in the backseat when he saw a cream-colored 1961 or 1962 Chevrolet "swerve around us" and shots were fired. He said there was "a minimum" of three persons in the Chevrolet.

"I tried to stop the car. I reached across Colonel Penn, who had fallen into the hands of Major Brown. I grabbed the top of the wheel. Colonel Penn was dead," Howard told the hushed courtroom.

"We knew what was in front of us so far as the firing was concerned, and we knew Athens was behind us. That's why we turned around at the bridge," Howard said.

Hudson seemed to grasp at straws on cross-examination. He disputed Howard's description of the car, saying Penn's companion had given a different description in an earlier statement to investigators. He called on Howard to identify the configuration of taillights on more than a dozen different kinds of cars. Howard's answers took on a tone of exasperation.

Then the young attorney asked the black army reserve officer:

"Did you use the regular restrooms at the service station in Atlanta?" Howard said yes and added that Brown did so also, but that no trouble was caused by it.

President Johnson had signed the Civil Rights Act of 1964 on July 2, but public accommodations, including service station restrooms, were still rigidly segregated in many parts of the South.

The prosecution moved from the killing itself to the accused killers and began forming its case to prove that Myers and Sims murdered Penn.

Mrs. Landys Miriam Moore, shy, middle-aged, a black dishwasher at the all-night Open House Restaurant on Hancock Street in Athens, testified she saw Sims, Herbert Guest, and others in the restaurant on the night of July 10 and they were "all wearing guns."

She said she saw no shotguns, only pistols. She further said the

men had come into the restaurant carrying guns on several occasions during the ten days prior to the Penn killing.

Grover B. Epps, white, operator of the Open House Restaurant,
also testified the defendants came to his restaurant frequently and
were there between midnight and 3:00 A.M. on July 11. He said he
saw no firearms.

Then eighteen-year-old Thomas E. "Hoss" Folendore took the
stand. Stuttering as he spoke, he told of being at Guest's garage
when he saw Myers and Sims there with sawed-off shotguns with
pistol grips.

Clete Johnson ordered two sawed-off, double-barreled shotguns
with pistol grips brought into the courtroom, and he asked Folendore if the weapons were similar to the ones he had seen. The
witness agreed that they were.

Folendore said he lied when he boasted to Sims and Myers: "I got
me one tonight. I don't know what you all have been doing."

Sims told him it was none of his business, Folendore testified,
and the youth said he left. Folendore told newsmen outside the
courtroom that he was only "joking" when he said "I got me one
tonight. . . ." Up to this point, the state had been careful not to
refer to the Ku Klux Klan. But outside the courtroom, young
Folendore boasted he was a Klansman and proud of it. "I believe in
the principles of the United Knights of the Ku Klux Klan," he said.
"This murder case doesn't scare me."

Another witness, Claude Bennett, a former employee of the
garage, testified that he, too, saw Myers and Sims at the garage
early on July 11 and that Sims was carrying a sawed-off shotgun.

The last of twelve witnesses to be put on the stand Tuesday,
September 1, was FBI agent Jack Simpson, who testified he had
twice formally interviewed James S. Lackey, first on July 29 and
again on August 6. Simpson said the last time he had a conversation with Lackey, the suspect offered to make a statement.

Simpson said he made no threats, offered Lackey no rewards, and
advised him of his rights before Lackey made the statement.

As Simpson was about to read the statement, defense attorney
Hudson leaped to his feet with objections. Judge Skelton ordered
the jury out of the room.

Hudson objected that Lackey was not on trial, that the state had failed to connect Lackey to Sims and Myers, and that therefore there was no legal basis for allowing the statement to be used as evidence.

Judge Skelton said he would take Hudson's objections under advisement, and he adjourned court for the day.

Lackey's confession could be the clincher that put Sims and Myers away, and everyone in the courtroom knew it.

Clete Johnson huddled with Jeff Wayne and decided the state would try to prove a conspiracy involving Lackey with Sims and Myers before trying again to get Lackey's statement admitted.

The Ku Klux Klan was at last about to become a part of the trial record of Howard Sims and Cecil Myers.

The next day, a policeman testified that he knew the defendants as members of the Ku Klux Klan. That brought an avalanche of objections from Hudson. There was more testimony. Not only were they members of the Klan, but they were seen together frequently, and they were usually armed. The conspiracy theory had been constructed, and the KKK and lethal weapons were part of it.

On September 2, 1964, special prosecutor Jeff Wayne, in a booming voice, read the confession that Lackey had given Simpson. The crowded courtroom was suddenly still and silent. Sims and Myers stared straight ahead. Lackey was not in the courtroom.

"I, James S. Lackey, make the following voluntary statement to Jack R. Simpson and Clarence A. Brom who I know to be special agents of the Federal Bureau of Investigation.

"I have been told by special agent Simpson that I need not make a statement and that I can consult an attorney prior to making any statement.

"I know that this may be used against me in court, no threats or promises have been made to me to get me to make this statement.

"On the morning of July 11, 1964, I was driving Cecil Myers' cream Chevy station wagon accompanied by Cecil Myers and Howard Sims.

"At some time between 4 A.M. and 4:30 A.M. we spotted a 1959 Chevy occupied by several colored men. We trailed the car and noticed the Washington, D.C., plates. This was on Thomas Street.

"I believe Mr. Sims said, 'That must be some of President Johnson's boys.'

"We saw this car for the first time headed north on Thomas Street, Route 29 and 72 through Athens. At either the intersection of Hancock or Daugherty streets is where I believe the remark was made by Cecil Myers to follow the car.

"I was driving and I began following the car as directed by Myers who was sitting alongside me up front. Sims was sitting in the back.

"Sims told me to fall back and follow the Negroes and I stayed back about one or two hundred yards.

"We went out 29 and 72 and on to 172 highway near Colbert, Georgia.

"I asked the others what they were going to do and Sims said, 'I'm going to kill me a nigger.' Myers indicated he would help Sims.

"Both Sims and Myers told me when to pass the car occupied by Negroes from Washington, D.C.

"When I was alongside the Negroes' car, both Myers and Sims fired shotguns into the Negroes' car.

"I drove on by the Negro car and turned around and came back.

"I didn't see the car into which the shots were fired as we returned from the area of the bridge to Athens.

"Herbert Guest and a boy named 'Horsefly' were at the garage when we arrived. Denver Phillips was also at the garage when we arrived...

"The two guns used in the shooting were shotguns. The double-barreled shotgun used by Cecil Myers was the shotgun that usually hangs on the wall of Guest's Garage. The shotgun used by Sims is his own gun which he placed in the Chevy II earlier in the evening.

"As soon as we got back to Guest's garage both Myers and Sims cleaned the shotguns in the garage. They wiped the guns off with a rag.

"Guest asked what had happened and Sims said, 'We shot one but don't know if we killed him or not.'

"The original reason for our following the colored men was because we had heard that Martin Luther King might make Georgia a testing ground with the civil rights bill. We thought some out-of-town niggers might stir up some trouble in Athens.

"We had intended scaring off any out-of-town colored people before they could give us any trouble. When the Washington, D.C., car was spotted on 7/11/64 we thought they might be out-of-towners who might cause trouble.

"Sims and Myers kept insisting that I follow the car from Washington, D.C. They had me go out of town so it would not look like someone from Athens did the shooting.

"I had no idea that they would really shoot the Negro and was very surprised when two shots were fired. Sims fired one shot and Myers fired one shot.

"Right away after the shots were fired, I drove across a bridge and up a hill and turned around. I didn't see what happened to the Negroes' car but Sims and Myers said it was swaying all over the road.

"We turned around and I drove straight back to Athens, cleaned the guns, then went to the Open House Restaurant for coffee.

"I saw only two people in the car from Washington, D.C., and didn't look at it after the shots were fired because I was busy driving.

"I learned what had happened between 11 A.M. and 12 noon on 7/11/64. I was surprised when I learned that the colored man had been killed near Colbert, Georgia. I didn't think Sims and Myers had actually killed the man.

"I said to myself, 'Those sonofabitches killed that man.'

"I have read this eight-page statement and it is true and correct.

"Signed: James S. Lackey. Witnessed by: Simpson and Brom."

There was suddenly whispering and mumbling in the courtroom. Sheriff Seagraves stood and looked around. Judge Skelton banged his gavel. Order was restored. The trial continued.

The state moved crisply to clinch its case against Sims and Myers.

Herbert Guest, the Athens garage operator and Ku Klux Klansman, was summoned to the stand.

"Speak a little louder," Judge Skelton ordered. Guest raised his voice slightly and continued:

"Well, I had three hours sleep the day before and I stayed with them [the FBI] until two or three o'clock. And I had promised them that I would come back the next evening and meet at six o'clock. I went home that first day they had me, and I slept three hours, and I went to work at three o'clock. I worked straight through till eleven or around ten-thirty the next day.

"They come out to the house before I got a shower, took a bath or [had] anything to eat and picked me up and carried me, and I blacked out or something happened to me at the Post Office and the questions that I give them — the statement that I give the FBI. I don't think that that ought to go against me because I don't remember nothing about it," Guest sputtered.

Guest claimed he had been spitting blood, that he had hurt his ankle when he fell on the steps of the courthouse, that he had lost fifty pounds since his arrest. Finally, he identified his initials on the statement.

Yes, Guest said, Sims, Myers and Lackey had been with him on the night of the shooting at the Open House Restaurant and later at his garage. Yes, they left and returned at dawn. Yes, he and the other owned sawed-off shotguns. Yes, Guest had talked with FBI agents on several occasions.

Here the garage operator paused.

"Did you give them a statement?" Jeff Wayne demanded.

"I give them a statement, but I don't know what they got in it," Guest mumbled.

"Is that your signature?" snapped Wayne as he shoved several typewritten pages before Guest.

"Can I get over here and speak to my lawyer and ask him something?" Guest said, looking frantically toward Hudson. The two men whispered briefly, then Guest began testifying about the statement.

"They picked me up on that day and I had to sign it," Guest all but murmured.

When Jeff Wayne returned to the subject of Myers, Sims, and Lackey, Guest followed his lawyer's advice.

"I will take the Fifth Amendment on that," he said. "I ain't answering anymore."

With Hudson pounding him with objections, Jeff Wayne tried to hammer away at Guest with a series of questions relating to the morning Penn was killed. Guest refused to answer on Fifth Amendment grounds.

FBI agents William Watry and Arthur Hamilton were then called to testify that they had taken certain statements from Guest. Defense attorney Hudson offered a flurry of objections aimed at keeping a second incriminating statement from being placed before the jury, knowing how damaging the Lackey confession had been. He failed.

On cross-examination, Hudson demanded of the agents why Guest had been taken to the Athens Post Office for interrogation without his shoes. The agents said he preferred to go barefoot, but that his shoes were later brought to him.

Finally, Wayne succeeded in reading Guest's statement to the jury.

"...On July 11, 1964, I had been at the Open House Restaurant in Athens, Georgia, between one and two A.M. with Cecil Myers, Howard Sims, and James Lackey, around 2 or 2:30 A.M. [I] returned to my garage, known as Guest's Garage, 423 East Hancock Avenue in Athens.

"They [Myers, Sims, Lackey] left in Cecil Myers' 1969 Chevy II station wagon. When they go off in this wagon, Lackey normally drives but I don't know how they were seated in the car when they left that morning around 2:30 A.M. From that time until around 5 A.M., I did not see them.

"I remained at the garage during the period, working on different jobs. Around 4:15 A.M., a Tom Stevens from Lawrenceville, Georgia, drove in, in his 1960 white automobile to get his boat trailer which was in my garage hitched to his car. I put a ball on the hitch to his car, put the trailer on and hooked up the taillights to the car. This took thirty to forty five minutes... I got a cup of coffee out of the vending machine at the station and Stevens had something to drink," Guest's statement continued.

"While at the station at around 5 A.M. I saw the Chevy II station wagon coming south on Thomas Street, then turning east on Hancock and to a place in front of the garage. I don't recall who was driving but I do recall seeing Howard Sims in the back seat. I remained in the [adjoining service station] with Stevens and finished my coffee. I then returned to my garage which was five minutes after seeing the station wagon make the above turn.

"As I entered my garage I saw Howard Sims hollering at Folendore, also known as Horsefly, and saying that Folendore should not be nosing in other people's business. Sims had a shotgun in his hand.

"Folendore had arrived at the garage, alone, a short time before, while I was finishing the work on Stevens' trailer. Nothing was said to me at this time as to where they had been, but when they left around 2:30 A.M. they told me that they were going over to Lackey's house to 'look for a cop.' Somebody said, 'Let's get breakfast,' and I agreed. Lackey, Sims, and Myers got into my car and I drove them to the Open House. We all had breakfast, leaving there about 5:30 A.M. We all got in my car and drove to the Klavern, 199½ Prince Avenue, Athens, Georgia, where Sims got out to get his car which was parked there.

"I then drove Lackey and Myers to my garage and they left for home in Myers' car. In addition to Folendore, Claude Bennett and Denver Phillips were at the garage around 5 A.M. Phillips was asleep in a car during the time.

"On the following Sunday morning, July 12, Cecil Myers and Sims were talking in front of my garage. I overheard one of them say that they thought the car had gone into the river and missed the bridge as they had not seen it all the way back to Athens. On Monday night, July 13th, sometime after dark, I heard Sims and Cecil Myers' conversation at my garage. While I listened, they talked about the murder of Penn. At this time they told me they were the ones that shot at the car in which Penn was killed. I don't know which one said what, but this is what they told me.

"Lackey was driving the Chevy II with Cecil Myers in the right front and Howard Sims in the rear. They told me about following the Penn car out of Athens, a good distance behind, and passing it just before they got to the Broad River bridge. They fired two or three shots at the car as they passed and at that time thought the car had gone into the river. They drove five or ten miles further, turned around and came back to Athens.

"The reason that they thought that the car had gone into the river was that they did not see it on the return trip. During this conversation, Sims said, 'I wonder if that policeman in Colbert recognized us,' indicating that they had seen him going through Colbert. I don't know if this was going up or on the return trip. I know that Billy Smith, the Colbert policeman, knows Sims and he may know Myers and Lackey. Smith has worked at different jobs around Athens, including filling stations, which would put him in a position to know Myers and Lackey. At this time I asked them if they had used the shotgun which I kept in my office. They denied it. I asked them this several times and each time they have denied it. I felt that Myers had taken my gun from my office on two occasions prior to Penn's murder. Myers had taken my shotgun from my office without my permission and I have repeatedly told him not to take it without me knowing it. One time I let him take it when the three of them were looking for a prowler at Lackey's house. The gun that I had in my office on July 11 is the Ithaca twelve-gauge, serial No. 24266.

"I had no reason to and did not check for the presence of this gun during the early morning hours of July 11. The second night after Denver Phillips was interviewed, Sims was at the garage quizzing Phillips concerning his interview. Denver was reluctant to answer and Sims said, 'If I go up the creek on this one there will be a lot of sons of bitches go up the creek before I do.'

"Sims also has stated since that time that he and Myers were concerned over Lackey cracking," the statement concluded.

The statement was signed by Guest and attested to by three FBI agents.

Two sawed-off shotguns with pistol grips were then identified and entered into evidence. There was technical testimony from Dr. Larry Howard, director of the Georgia State Crime Laboratory, and from FBI firearms identification expert Robert Zimmer that indicated the blast that killed Penn could have come from either of the two shotguns.

Wayne entered into evidence a long series of photographs and other physical evidence taken from the scene. At noon, Thursday, September 3, the state rested its case after twenty-five witnesses had given testimony for the previous three days.

The most damaging blows were Lackey's confession and Guest's statement, which corroborated much of what Lackey had told the FBI. Seemingly, the state had put together a textbook case of murder against Sims and Myers.

10 • The Defense

JIM HUDSON opened for the defense by calling Howard Sims to the stand.

"Your honor, please, the defendant Howard Sims will make an unsworn statement at this time. Take the stand, Mr. Sims. Turn around and listen to the judge, and he will advise you of your rights."

Judge Skelton instructed Sims that under Georgia law, at the time, a defendant in a capital case could make an unsworn statement and was not subject to cross-examination. (This unsworn statement law was later ruled unconstitutional.)

Sims spoke deliberately and calmly:

"My name is Joseph Howard Sims. I live at 230 Gilliland Drive, in Athens, Georgia. I have lived in Athens all my life except what time I was in the service. I am innocent of this. I had nothing to do with the killing of Lemuel Penn. I understand that the act happened around five o'clock in the morning of July 11, and I believe that I was in Athens at that time. I had never seen Lemuel Penn, and I don't know whether he had ever seen me, but I had nothing whatsoever to do with his killing. I am completely innocent of the crime."

Then it was Myers' turn. He appeared nervous and less confident than Sims. He was in a hurry to get it over with.

"My name is Cecil William Myers. I am the father of three children and am expecting another one soon. I can assure you that I had nothing to do with this killing of Lemuel Penn. I believe that it is said that it happened about five o'clock in the morning, and I do believe that I was in town, in Athens at this time. I have lived in Athens only a short while and I can assure you that I had nothing to do with this." Myers left the stand quickly and returned to the defendants' table.

Next, Hudson turned his attention to the confession of James Lackey. He placed on the stand John W. (Billy) Williford, one of Lackey's court-appointed lawyers. Williford swore that Lackey had repudiated the confession with another sworn statement on August 27. Hudson read the repudiation to the jury:

"To the Madison County grand jury and to the federal grand jury of the Middle District of Georgia, August 21, 1964.

"I James Spurgeon Lackey, at this time, would like to call your attention that all statements made to the Federal Bureau of Investigation agents implicating, namely, Cecil Myers and Howard Sims, and Herbert Guest and any others, have been made under fears and threats. After harassment for a period of thirty days with the loss of sleep and continued interrogation, after this my mental condition was at its lowest ebb and was only glad to make any statements or sign anything. My wife went through a miscarriage because of all this pressure and continued intimidation. I was told by the federal investigator Simpson that if I gave help to arrest or convict the killers of William [sic] Penn, that the federal government would see that I was well taken care of at all times.

"He told me that in cases such as this that the government had started with a $3,000 reward and had gone higher. I would like to be called before the grand jury and repudiate all the statements that have been made or signed by me because of my mental condition at this time.

"I am making this statement within my own power. I am under no threats or duress. I am doing this to clear my own conscience for the harm I have done my co-defendants."

The statement was signed by Lackey and eight witnesses.

(Nearly fifteen years later, Lackey's other attorney, Nick Chilivis, now a successful criminal lawyer in Atlanta, recalled Lackey's confession and repudiation. "He just repudiated the statement. He said he had been harassed and intimidated. But he never did say the statement was not true," Chilivis chuckled.)

Hudson called as a witness an Athens psychiatrist, Dr. James Jordan, who testified that Lackey had a "low borderline IQ of 90" and that he was "a paranoid personality."

"He told me that in the service station at times he had caught people staring at him," Dr. Jordan testified. "He knew what they were thinking about; that they were looking at his head, but he never said anything to them."

The psychiatrist also recounted what Lackey had told him about the FBI's attempts to induce him to sign a confession.

"Well, essentially Mr. Lackey told me that different approaches had been used to get some of this information from him. As I recall, one thing he said was 'they tried this buddy-buddy stuff on me and that didn't work.' Another approach was they tried money and that didn't work, and then they told him that his friends were putting his neck in a noose."

On cross-examination, Dr. Jordan admitted that Lackey was not mentally incompetent.

Hudson called only two more defense witnesses, Mrs. Ruth Bertling and Clyde Harper, both of whom testified they saw the defendants in the Open House Restaurant shortly before or at 5:00 A.M. on July 11.

Hudson had himself placed under oath, and told of driving the twenty-four miles from the Open House Restaurant to the bridge over the Broad River. The trip took, he said, thirty-one minutes.

The state had spent three and one-half days putting together its case against Sims and Myers. The defense used less than two hours trying to prove the innocence of the two men.

It was time to close.

Solicitor General Clete Johnson delivered the first closing argument. He reviewed the evidence point by point. He declared the state had proved beyond any reasonable doubt that the defendants had murdered Lemuel Penn early on the morning of July 11 in Madison County.

"It was just as much an assassination as it was when President Kennedy was shot down," Johnson told the jury. He asked that Sims and Myers be put to death for the crime which had no motive other than "hate and violence."

"Lemuel Penn was born a Negro. He came into this world with black skin. Is that a crime? Would that justify taking a shotgun and blowing his head off because he is black?" Johnson asked the all-white jury.

He referred to Sims and Myers as "nightriders looking for trouble and trying to take the law into their own hands. . . Now, gentlemen, that is not right. Something ought to be done to stop this nightriding with pistols and shotguns."

He urged the jury to return a verdict that "will not be the ridicule of this county."

"The honor of the great state of Georgia is on trial here today!" he shouted. He accused Sims and Myers of bringing their wives and children to court during the trial "for the purpose of creating sympathy with the jury," and he said the families would be better off not living with murderers.

When the jury filed out for recess at the close of Johnson's argument, several spectators walked up to Johnson, shook his hand, and congratulated him on his presentation. Another who complimented him was defense attorney Jim Hudson.

The jury returned, and it was Hudson's turn. Scowling and pounding his fist on the rail in front of the jury box, Hudson declared, "This ain't no car-theft case, and this ain't no guitar-picking-on-Sunday case. This is a murder case."

The thirty-five-year old Athens attorney accused the FBI and state prosecutors of attempting to send Sims and Myers to the electric chair with circumstantial and irrelevant evidence and a confession that was not freely given. He reminded the jury that a psychiatrist had testified that James Lackey was mentally ill, "a man with a paranoid personality who doesn't trust anybody in the world.

"He thinks he has a misshapen head and thinks people stare at him and laugh. And he has completely repudiated everything he said in the statement," Hudson said.

He noted that FBI agent Jack Simpson admitted telling Lackey that the FBI sometimes pays as much as $3,000 for information in "complicated cases such as this."

"What do you think this meant to James Lackey, a mentally ill person working in a filling station?" Hudson demanded. "Lackey's confession is the only thing that remotely connects these men with the scene of the crime, and even he said it wasn't so."

The emotional high point of the closing came when John Darsey, the old war-crimes prosecutor turned court-appointed defense lawyer, rose to rail against the federal government.

He told the jury that FBI agents had been sent to Madison County to investigate the Penn murder and instructed, "Don't come back until you bring us white meat."

He roared at "the carpetbagging administration of justice." He attacked President Lyndon Johnson for sending "swarms" of FBI agents to this area and "infiltrating our land."

"Never let it be said," he shouted, "that a Madison County jury converted an electric chair into a sacrificial altar on which the pure flesh of a member of the human race was sacrificed to the savage, revengeful appetite of a raging mob."

Ringing his hands and mopping his brow with a sweat-soaked handkerchief, Darsey paced back and forth in front of the jury. He sometimes shouted so loudly that his words could not be clearly understood. In the midst of his speech, Darsey paused and apologized to the jury for being "overzealous."

Five times during his hour-long tirade, Darsey reminded the jurors that they were Anglo-Saxon. Once while charging that the federal government had set out specifically to get Sims and Myers, Darsey shouted:

"Fe fi fo fum! I smell the blood of an Englishman! Send 'em on, Mister President, send 'em on!"

Then he picked up a newspaper and read to the jury about a large number of FBI agents being sent into the area. Red-faced and panting, Darsey wheeled and shouted at FBI agent Robert Kane, who was seated at the prosecution table:

"When they couldn't get white meat, they built a sham of a case."

Finally, hoarse and gasping, Darsey finished his argument and all but collapsed into a chair at the defense table.

Jeff Wayne, the special prosecutor, took the floor with a different approach.

Speaking in a slow and sometimes soft tone, Wayne took thirty-one minutes to complete the state's concluding argument. The gaunt, forty-eight-year-old prosecutor reviewed the evidence once again. He referred to the Penn killing and several other acts of violence and intimidation against black people in the Athens area.

"Our laws are not made for the protection of one color or one race. Except for the grace of God, you could have been born of the colored race."

He termed the killing "a horrible thing" and said, "If this is tolerated, human life has reached the point — black or white — when it is not worth a ten-cent box of snuff."

During his argument, Wayne told the jury that Sims and Myers had been "going out on shooting sprees." Sims shook his head vigorously from side to side. Myers remained stoic.

Judge Skelton charged the jury concerning the law and penalties in murder cases.

The jury retired at 4:40 P.M. on Friday, September 4.

Two dozen blacks who had witnessed the trial from a small balcony over the courtroom silently walked from the building when the jury began deliberations, as if they already knew the verdict.

11 • The Verdict

JACK NELSON, Pulitzer Prize-winning reporter for *The Atlanta Constitution*, decided to interview Sims while waiting for the jury to return.

He wanted to know what the tough Klansman was thinking while a jury was deciding whether he would live or die; whether he would go to prison for years or remain free. But Sims wasn't interested in talking about that; he was furious at Nelson.

"You stink!" he said. "You ruined the best part of Athens! You destroyed some of the finest social and service clubs in town. I wouldn't talk to you about anything."

Sims was referring to a series of newspaper stories by Nelson four years earlier that dealt with illegal slot machines and other gambling devices in Athens veterans' clubs and other organizations.

Courtroom spectators were astonished that Sims could be so concerned about old news stories concerning slot machines when his own fate hung in the balance.

At 6:40 P.M. the jury suspended deliberations and piled into Georgia State Patrol cars to dine at a truckstop several miles out of town.

At 8:40 P.M. the jury resumed deliberations. Sims remained calm.

Shortly after ten P.M. the jury sent Judge Skelton word that it had reached a verdict. The judge took his place on the bench and warned against any outburst.

The jury filed into the box.

"Mr. Foreman and gentlemen of the jury, have you reached a verdict?" Judge Skelton asked.

The courtroom was crowded and hot and absolutely silent. "Let the clerk read and publish the verdict," said the judge.

Henry Snelling, clerk of the court, took the verdict from the jury foreman. Sims and Myers bowed their heads and closed their eyes. Snelling slowly read: "We, the jury, find the defendants, Joseph Howard Sims and Cecil Myers, not guilty."

A suppressed cry of jubilation and a single handclap split the air.

"Wait a minute!" Judge Skelton roared, raising his robed arm toward the crowd. "There will be no talking and no one shall move until court is adjourned."

The crowd waited a moment in silence. The jury filed out of the room; then the judge. Sheriff Dewey Seagraves announced, "Court is adjourned." It was 10:14 P.M.

Applause and some cheering erupted. Solicitor General Clete Johnson congratulated Sims and Myers on the verdict. "There was nothing personal in this," he said.

Sims said he had felt confident of the verdict, even before the trial began. "The verdict was the only one they could bring in and be fair," he said, adding that he had become concerned when the jury went to supper without returning a verdict.

Myers appeared pale and shaken and refused to talk to newsmen. Sims's wife wept. "I'm overjoyed. I have prayed for this," she said, looking gratefully toward her husband.

The two defendants, their attorneys, several police officers, and a dozen well-wishers went across the street from the red-brick courthouse to the office of attorney Hap Boggs to pose for pictures and to celebrate.

Among those congratulating Sims and Myers were several of their fellow Ku Klux Klansmen.

Finally the courtroom was silent and almost empty. The floor was littered with paper and cigarette butts. Benches and chairs were shoved askew. Even the crowd that had gathered in town to await the verdict broke up.

An electric clock advertising a soft drink over the judge's bench pointed almost to midnight.

"It's just like after a storm," said Sheriff Seagraves as he looked over the empty courtroom.

The jury at the outset voted eleven to one for acquittal. "One fellow was a little slow making up his mind," said a juror, explaining why the panel was out so long.

More than fourteen years later, an attorney connected with the case recalled that the defense was certain of victory, no matter what evidence was presented. "The jury had been checked out. Two-thirds of them were either members of the Klan or known to be sympathetic to the Klan," he said. A list of jurors was passed among defense attorneys. A dot beside a juror's name indicated he was either a member of the KKK or pro-Klan.

On the night following the verdict, at a rally of the National Knights of the Ku Klux Klan at Stone Mountain, Georgia, Imperial Wizard James Venable declared: "You'll never be able to convict a white man that killed a nigger that encroaches on the white race in the South."

The United Klans of America, Knights of the Ku Klux Klan held a banquet in nearby Lawrenceville to celebrate the acquittal of Sims and Myers. Among the guests of honor was Madison County Sheriff Seagraves.

12 • Heroes and Black Shirts

SIMS AND MYERS, still facing federal civil rights charges, were released on $25,000 bond each four days after their acquittal.

Lackey, still facing murder and civil rights conspiracy charges, was unable to make bail. He remained in jail until January 7, 1965, and was finally released on $10,000 bond. Lackey was never tried for murder.

Meanwhile, Sims and Myers became heroes of the Klan. They were welcomed at rallies, cross-burnings, and demonstrations. They showed up in Americus in southwest Georgia, where racial tensions were running high.

They came to Atlanta and marched with ranking KKK leaders in a giant "states' rights" parade organized by Lester Maddox in January 1965. Within two years Maddox would become governor of Georgia.

Sims and Myers were arrested on charges of creating a disturbance, and money was collected for their legal defense throughout the South. No accurate accounting of how much Klansmen paid for that defense was ever reported.

Sims and Myers also became disenchanted with Grand Dragon Calvin Craig's United Klans of America. Craig talked too much, acted too little, they felt. They were interested in action.

They organized an outfit called the Black Knights of the Ku Klux Klan. They wore black clothing with military-like insignias. They continued to brandish guns and clubs. They continued to be involved in racial turmoil and incidents of violence and near-violence.

A typical incident occurred near Crawfordville in Taliaferro County, Georgia, in 1965.

Racial unrest had spread that year to this middle Georgia county. Blacks marched and sang and demanded integration of the small rural county's school system. And they won their rights.

Then the "Black Shirt Boys" came. With them came more trouble.

George Turner, a black farmer, would later testify under oath that on October 17, 1965, he was driving on a desolate county road, on his way to a church service, when two cars forced him to stop.

"I said, 'Man, what in the world are you doing?' they started jumping out of the cars with shotguns and pistols and rifles...white men, all dressed in black," he testified.

One man walked up to Turner's car and began cursing and striking Turner with his hands. About that time, Turner said, his brother, Omer, who was following him to church in another car, arrived on the scene and began crying, "That's my baby brother. Don't y'all hurt him, please."

"Don't let that damn nigger get out. Stop him," one of the men yelled, according to Omer Turner.

Then one Black Shirt fired a shot near Omer and told him, "If you'll get back, we'll stop."

Omer said, "I took one step back — and they stopped and left. They were all dressed just alike, with sawed-off shotguns, pistols and clubs."

In court, George Turner identified the man who beat him as Cecil William Myers; Omer Turner identified the man who fired the shot as Joseph Howard Sims.

The Turner brothers had lived in Taliaferro County all their lives. They were not involved in any civil rights activities.

The Turners reported their encounter to Sheriff Milton Moore, who went looking for "the Black Shirt Boys" and found their car. In their auto he found six sawed-off shotguns, four pistols with holsters, a .22 rifle, several bandoliers of shotgun and pistol ammunition, a chain with a handle on it, and four wooden clubs with "KKK" and Nazi swastikas carved in their handles.

The sheriff said he asked the Black Shirts to leave the county.

"Your face must be black just like the rest of them," one of the Black Shirts told the sheriff. The lawman identified him as Joseph Howard Sims.

13 • Tragedy Strikes Again

IN MAY 1966, the life of Joseph Howard Sims, the defender of the white race against black encroachment, took a bizarre turn.

Sims shot his wife.

Sims was a skilled auto mechanic and machinist, but he had difficulty finding employment after his acquittal in the killing of Colonel Penn. He thought he was home free at one stage, when Federal District Judge William A. Bootle threw out a federal grand jury indictment against him and others. That indictment charged that they violated Colonel Penn's civil rights by killing him. Bootle's ruling did not stick. The Supreme Court reversed that decision, and Sims and his friends once again were awaiting trial, this time in a federal court.

The strain was getting to the forty-five-year-old Sims. He already was noted in Athens for his bad temper. It got worse.

His thirty-five-year-old wife was working double shifts as a nurse's aide in Athens General Hospital to support Sims, herself, and their eight children. The burden was too heavy. Their marriage fell apart.

About two weeks after their separation, Mrs. Sims took time out from her duties in the hospital maternity ward to speak with her brother on the phone. When she hung up, she looked up and saw Sims.

He asked her to come into the corridor to speak with him for a moment. Mrs. Sims refused.

Sims suddenly drew a pistol, leveled it at her and fired twice. The first bullet missed; the second struck her in the face.

Sims wheeled and ran through the room reserved for women in labor. A laundryman in the hospital at the time chased him down three flights of stairs. But the Ku Klux Black Shirt jumped into a 1948 Chevrolet and fled.

Police said later that the car was "loaded with guns."

Lawmen combed the countryside for a day and a half. They suspected Sims would try to get in touch with one of his buddies in the Klan. They were right.

Sims called a Klansman friend south of Atlanta and made arrangements to surrender to Butts County Sheriff J. D. Pope. Sims refused to come to the sheriff's office, so arrangements were made for a rendezvous with the sheriff in the rural countryside.

After Sims's surrender a deputy told newsmen that Sims seemed relieved "because he found out that his wife was going to be all right. He just talked like nothing had happened."

Sims was charged with assault with intent to murder. A few days later he was admitted to Milledgeville State Hospital for psychiatric evaluation.

It was a troublesome time not only for Sims, but for Herbert Guest. Inspectors for the Food and Drug Administration brought charges against Guest alleging that he had possessed and sold illegal amphetamines at his garage. Guest immediately entered a plea of not guilty.

Then the inspectors showed up in court to testify that, posing as students, they had purchased "pep pills." Guest recognized the undercover men and changed his plea to guilty.

14 • Another Try

WHILE SIMS, Myers and their Klan pals continued to harass and intimidate blacks with seeming impunity, white Athens, Georgia, and environs rolled over and went back to sleep.

Department of Justice attorneys, however, were determined to try again to prosecute the accused killers of Lemuel Penn and their cohorts. A federal grand jury in Athens returned a civil rights indictment on October 16, 1964, against Sims, Myers, Guest, and Lackey, plus two other Klansmen — Denver Phillips and George Hampton Turner. The indictments were based on the recently enacted Civil Rights Act of 1964 and another civil rights law enacted in 1870. The indictments alleged that the defendants systematically attempted to deprive blacks of their civil rights, guaranteed under federal law, by intimidation, including shooting, killing, and beating them, destroying their property, and pursuing them in cars.

Attorneys for the Klansmen immediately appealed to federal district court in Macon, asking that the indictment be dismissed on grounds that no specific violations of federal law were alleged. Further, the defense contended, even if the allegations in the indictment were true, those allegations amounted to specific violations of state statutes and therefore were outside the jurisidiction of the federal courts.

Government attorneys were confident their true bill would be upheld. The trial of the Klansmen was scheduled for January 11, 1964.

Federal district Judge William A. Bootle threw out the indictment, ruling the federal court could not "usurp" jurisdiction where it has none.

"The enforcement of general criminal laws is a local matter with authority and responsibility resting squarely with local and state officials," the judge said.

Then the sixty-two-year-old Bootle added, "Fortunately, under the Criminal Appeals Act. . . the federal government has a speedy remedy for a review of this ruling by the Supreme Court."

Six months later, the Supreme Court agreed to hear the government's appeal in its new term, beginning October 4, 1965.

In a decision on March 28, 1966, the U.S. Supreme Court reversed Judge Bootle (*U. S. v. Guest*) and upheld the rights of the federal government to try the defendants under Section 241 of Title 18 of the United States Code (Conspiracy Against Rights of Citizens), which reads:

"If two or more persons conspire to injure, oppress, threaten, or intimidate any citizen in the free exercise or enjoyment of any right or privilege secured to him by the Constitution or laws of the United States, or because of his so having exercised the same; or

"If two or more persons in disguise on the highway, or on the premises of another, with intent to prevent or hinder his free exercise or enjoyment of any right or privilege so secured—

"They shall be fined not more than $5,000 or imprisoned not more than ten years, or both."

The last barrier to another trial, this one in federal court, had been overcome.

15 • Last Chance for Justice

GRIM-FACED, his hands manacled, Howard Sims was brought into the federal courtroom in Athens on June 28, 1966, to stand trial once again for his involvement in the slaying of Lemuel Penn. With him was Cecil Myers, his companion on forays against blacks, and George Hampton, another member of the Ku Klux Klan.

Three others named in the federal indictment — James Lackey, Herbert Guest, and Denver Phillips — were to stand trial later.

The opening day of the trial was a sharp contrast to the opening day of court in Madison County nearly two years earlier, when Sims and Myers were acquitted of murdering Penn. There were no refreshments served on the lawn of the federal building. There was no idle chatter from the defendants about their hobbies or their plans for the future.

Stern-faced Federal District Judge William A. Bootle presided.

U.S. Attorney Floyd Buford of Macon represented the government.

Once again, young Jim Hudson of Athens represented the defense. The murder case in Madison County had been relatively easy for Hudson. He knew he had a popular cause and was working in sympathetic territory. He was not so certain here. Besides, the government already had a good idea of the defense's tactics.

In addition, Sims had been charged with attempted murder and was being held in the county jail. Hudson could hardly present his client as a peaceable, law-abiding citizen.

"We will show," said Buford in his opening argument, "that Cecil William Myers and Joseph Howard Sims actually took part in the slaying of Colonel Penn, a citizen of the United States.

"We are not trying Myers and Sims for murder," Buford said. "We are trying them for conspiracy. But in order to prove our conspiracy charge, we are going to prove to you that [Penn's murder] was part of that plan... It was part of a broad conspiracy to keep out-of-state Negroes from coming into the Athens area, and it was part of that conspiracy to run such Negroes out of the area."

In his forty-five-minute opening argument, Buford detailed a series of incidents which he said were a part of this organized scheme of intimidation by the three defendants and other Klansmen.

Hudson took a new tack for the defense. His clients weren't nightriding terrorists at all. "These poor country boys were simply trying to help people like you and me," he told the jury in his opening argument. "They conspired to keep racial violence from tearing Athens apart.... Since these boys got together, we haven't had racial violence in Athens.

"It [the evidence] will show that back in those times things were about to get out of hand, and it will show that these boys were willing to spend enough of their time and money to help you and me," Hudson continued.

"And now the government is trying to put them in the penitentiary. Mr. Buford will show some incidents. He will show that these boys wanted to keep Negroes in their place — he will probably show that. But the evidence will nowhere indicate that these people conspired to keep people from traveling interstate commerce."

Again and again, Hudson characterized his clients as protectors of Athens. He concluded his argument:

"They weren't doing it for money. They were doing it for you. They were doing it for me. They were doing it for your family and my family, to keep racial violence out of Athens, Georgia."

The government relied on most of the evidence used by the state in the Penn murder trial. It chose not to use Lackey's repudiated confession in the first federal court trial; it would be entered into evidence against Lackey in the second. Buford also called a surprise witness, Thomas (Big Tom) Stephens, who said he was a former Klansmen and a friend of Herbert Guest.

Stephens testified he had been told by Sims and Myers that they fired into a car with District of Columbia license plates on July 11, 1964, and had hoped the car would drive off a bridge and go into the river. It did not.

James "Preacher" Potts, Herbert Guest's black "gofer," testified about the time when he was sent on a bogus errand in March of 1964, only to be grabbed by hooded men, stretched across the hood of a car, and given eighteen lashes with a leather strap. He identified his assailants' spokesman as Howard Sims.

An Athens policeman told the jury how Sims had ordered a black couple in a car with New Jersey plates to "get your black asses back up North where you came from."

George and Omer Turner recounted their confrontation with the Black Shirt Boys in Taliaferro County. George Turner identified Myers as the man who beat him. Omer Turner identified Sims as the man who fired the shot.

Frank Gilmore of Athens told of being followed home by Klansmen and later arrested and held overnight by Athens police. Gilmore said he was never told why he had been placed in jail.

The government entered into evidence a Klan hood with red tassel, along with sawed-off shotguns and chains.

The case against Sims, Myers, and George Hampton Turner was concluded on Friday, July 2, 1965, after the jury listened to an impassioned plea from Jim Hudson.

"Don't convict them because they're mean men and don't like colored people and might have been guilty of a little — maybe bad — violence," Hudson beseeched the jury.

Hudson suggested that perhaps the reason Athens had experienced no racial trouble similar to the Watts riot was because blacks knew "somebody is around looking at them." Pointing to the defendants, Hudson said: "These boys sitting there, I submit, are one reason we haven't had any trouble."

Referring to the beating of Preacher Potts, Hudson admitted "it was a bad thing." But he said he doubted Potts could have identified anyone who had his face covered by a hood.

The defense attorney asked the jury not to convict Sims "of just cussin' " in the incident when Sims was supposed to have ordered out of town a black couple in a car with New Jersey tags. "When Sims said, 'You all get back to New Jersey,' one way of looking at that is, he was inviting them to use interstate commerce," Hudson said.

Buford had the last word to the jury. Brandishing a KKK hood, the government attorney declared: "These are brave men, but they have to peep from behind a cowardly thing like this."

As for the Potts beating, Buford said it was a case of Klansmen getting together and deciding "we can't go home tonight without whipping a nigger."

Buford reviewed the other incidents, and he asserted of the murder of Lemuel Penn: "We've got two men on trial here who participated in that killing."

The jury began deliberations at 4:12 P.M. It returned its verdict at 1:55 A.M. Judge Bootle ordered the verdict sealed and kept secret until after the trial of Guest, Lackey, and Phillips the following week.

That second trial followed much the pattern of the first, except that Lackey's confession was entered into evidence by the government over the strenuous objections of the defense. James Lackey, Herbert Guest, and Denver Phillips were acquitted by the second jury. The verdict in the first trial was unsealed, and it turned out that George Hampton Turner was also acquitted.

Joseph Howard Sims and Cecil William Myers were both found guilty.

Myers and Sims showed no emotion. "This isn't over yet," Myers told a newsman.

On the following morning, Myers and Sims heard their sentences pronounced by Judge Bootle — ten years each in the federal penitentiary.

Myers was released on appeal bond; Sims was held in the Clarke County jail on the attempted murder charge. On July 19, 1966, he

pleaded guilty in Clarke County superior court to a charge of
assault with intent to kill his estranged wife. He was given another
ten-year sentence, this time by Superior Court Judge James Barrow,
the man who two years earlier had been about the only local
elected official to offer to assist the FBI in its investigation of the
Penn murder case, the man who had been accused by other local
leaders of "overreacting" to the activities of the Ku Klux Klan in
Athens, Georgia.

16 • The Surviving Personae

BY JULY OF 1979, the fifteenth anniversary of the Lemuel Penn murder, James Lackey, Cecil Myers, Herbert Guest, and Howard Sims were all free men.

Lackey never served a day in prison. He moved with his family from Athens to work as "a chicken catcher" in a poultry-processing operation near Gainesville, Georgia.

Herbert Guest served very little time on the illegal-drug charge. His sentence expired December 21, 1967, and he returned to Athens with his liberty completely intact, not even under a parole officer's supervision. He returned also to the garage business, but only briefly. By the early 1970s, Guest was in trouble with federal drug agents again, this time on new charges of distribution of amphetamines. Again indicted and convicted, Guest was sentenced on November 30, 1972, to five years in prison to be followed by a court-mandated "special" parole of fifteen years and an $11,000 fine. Guest appealed his conviction and sentence but lost. In January of 1974 he surrendered to federal authorities and began his sentence in the federal penitentiary at Atlanta. He was released in December of 1976. Guest returned to Athens and in July 1979 was employed by his wife Blanche, who had purchased the Open House

Restaurant — the same cafe where armed Klansmen more than fifteen years earlier had gathered to plot and hate.

Cecil William Myers was sentenced to serve a portion of his time at the federal penitentiary at Terre Haute, Indiana. He was assigned to the prison mill there and worked as a loom fixer. Myers was divorced while in prison. He also was denied parole but was later transferred to the minimum-security federal prison facility at Eglin Air Force Base, Florida, where he was released under supervision of federal probation authorities on June 9, 1972. Myers returned to northeast Georgia and worked for a time as a truckdriver and skilled textile machinist in mills in both Georgia and South Carolina. He reportedly also acquired a new skill as a brickmason. He was released from all federal supervision on December 19, 1975.

Joseph Howard Sims was first sent to the Georgia State Prison at Reidsville for the shooting of his wife. At the end of that state sentence, he was transferred to federal authorities to begin serving time for the civil rights offense on December 31, 1970. He began his sentence at Terre Haute and was later transferred to Atlanta. His wife divorced him while he was in prison.

Prison officials described Sims as "an extremely intelligent man." He worked at a variety of machine shop assignments and took advanced courses in automobile mechanics. He also was denied parole. On October 20, 1976, Sims had built enough "good time" for mandatory release and returned to Athens, Georgia, where he lived and worked under the supervision of federal probation authorities. Despite his other skills, Sims settled on becoming a truckdriver.

A federal officer said Sims showed "a markedly improved attitude" upon his release from prison. But his attorney, Jim Hudson, warned this author that it might be dangerous to try to interview Sims.

In the fall of 1978, Sims sent a message through his probation officer to Robert Kane, his old adversary whom he had once threatened to kill and who now was an official with the Georgia State Department of Revenue.

What was the message?

"He said he wanted his guns back," Kane reported.

POSTSCRIPT

Joseph Howard Sims, 58 and a semi-invalid, met death on the night of June 1, 1981. He was shot once in the chest at a flea market just outside Athens. Edward U. Skinner, whom authorities identified as a friend of Sims, was charged with murder. The death weapon was a 12-gauge shotgun—the same kind of gun that ended the life of Lemuel Penn.

EPILOGUE
A Cancer
in Remission

Lemuel Penn and the others across the South who died and suffered at the hands of the Ku Klux Klan in the mid-1960s did not do so in vain. The atrocities perpetrated against innocent victims turned national attention, more than ever, to the injustices present in the South. And law-abiding Southerners increasingly came to despise the nightriders and what they stood for.

Shortly after Penn was murdered, U.S. Rep. Charles Longstreet Weltner, D-Atlanta, called on the House Committee on Un-American Activities to launch a full-scale investigation of the Klan and Klan violence. The committee at first was reluctant to probe the Klan.

But violence continued in the South and, finally and reluctantly, HUAC Chairman Edwin E. Willis of Louisiana ordered that full-scale investigation of the Klan. A series of public hearings on Klan activities began on October 19, 1965, and ended February 25, 1966. Dozens of Klansmen and KKK leaders were called to testify. A few cooperated; most did not. They sat under the hot lights and squirmed and took the Fifth Amendment when asked about their activities.

Despite this, a clear picture of Klan violence emerged: how the

Klan cheated its members, how it spread hatred and spawned violence, how it encouraged the purchase and use of firearms.

At the close of the committee's investigative session of February 24, 1966, Congressman Weltner pointed out that most of the members of the subcommittee conducting the Klan hearings were Southerners. The congressman from Atlanta appealed to citizens of the South to examine the committee's findings and determine "whether or not the Klan is going to govern community affairs in the South, or whether it will be the people of the South." Said Weltner: "The challenge now passes from the Congress and it is placed directly into the hands of the people of the South. I for one am confident that Southern people are anxious to make their own decisions; that they desire the democratic process to be operative; and they desire the problems of the South, however pressing and compelling they may be, be determined within the framework of the Constitution of the United States, in accordance with the laws of the United States and the free expression of public opinion.

"I do not really believe that Southerners really want to turn those decisions over to any group of hooded, hidden, terroristic, anonymous men."

A few months later, Weltner stepped aside as congressman. He refused to seek re-election, saying he did not wish his name to appear on the same ticket with that of Lester Maddox, the segregationist Democratic candidate for governor who handed out pick-handled "nigger knockers" as campaign souvenirs. At the time in Georgia, Democratic party rules required every nominee on the ticket to support the entire ticket.

Nevertheless, Weltner and his colleagues on HUAC performed a national and regional service by focusing attention on the Klan. "We really didn't turn up any new information," Weltner said years later. "But we put the whole problem into perspective. We showed the scope of Klan activities in the South."

More important, HUAC made Klan leaders uncomfortable. Several were indicted for contempt of Congress for their refusal to answer questions put to them by the committee. Robert Shelton of Tuscaloosa, Alabama, imperial wizard of the United Klans of America, Knights of the Ku Klux Klan, was sent to prison for refusing to answer questions.

Suddenly, there were reports across the South of Klaverns being disbanded, of Klan leaders resigning en masse and some even having changes of heart. Georgia Grand Dragon Calvin Craig resigned from the United Klans and became a member of the integrated board of directors of the Atlanta Model Cities Program that promoted new and refurbished biracial residential projects.

By the end of the decade of the sixties, the Klan had apparently petered out in the South. "I really don't know what we did," said Weltner, "except the Klan leadership did not like to sit under public scrutiny and answer questions about their activities. And they knew if they refused to answer, they could go to prison. So they just quit the Klan."

The civil rights movement gave way to the Vietnam War protests, which ultimately saw an end to that unpopular conflict in southeast Asia. The long-hairs and the flower children came and went. President Richard Nixon, who had built his reputation as a hardline anti-Communist, introduced the nation to detente with the Soviet Union and reopened relations with Red China.

Then Nixon fell in the disgrace of Watergate. A liberal Southerner, Jimmy Carter, came to the White House in 1976. Faith in the country's future seemed renewed for a time.

As the decade wore on, energy became scarcer and more expensive. Whites, sensing the growing economic competition for better jobs by blacks, hurled charges of reverse discrimination against employers and the government. Schools became resegregated as whites fled from the cities to the suburbs.

Sporadic reports of violence and cross-burnings began to crop up in the headlines. A new generation of Klan leaders began to go public, one even proclaiming he intended to seek the presidency. Some of the old generation, frightened into inactivity a decade earlier by the glare of public attention, came out of the closet. Calvin Craig abandoned any pretense of joining in a coalition with blacks and liberal whites. He again became a chief organizer for the United Klans of America.

Klansmen publicly announced they had organized "guerrilla welfare" schools all across the South to train their members in the use of firearms and terror tactics "against the niggers."

Klan-inspired violence erupted across the nation from New

England to Florida and North Carolina.

Unlike the hooded nightriders of the 1960s, the new Klansmen were not afraid to show their faces. They held press conferences and public ceremonies and even had the temerity to endorse Ronald Reagan for president, although he repudiated their endorsement.

An American cancer was no longer in remission. It was growing again and it was as malignant as ever.

After a decade and a half of impotence and silence, partly caused by the murder of Lemuel A. Penn, the Ku Klux Klan was back in business and flourishing.

Suggested Reading

Compiled by Edward A. Hatfield

CONTEMPORARY RELEVANCE

Levitas, Daniel. *The Terrorist Next Door: The Militia Movement and the Radical Right*. New York: St. Martin's Press, 2002.

Romano, Renee C. *Racial Reckoning: Prosecuting America's Civil Rights Murders*. Cambridge: Harvard University Press, 2014.

Williams, Chad; Kidada Williams, and Keisha Blain, eds. *The Charleston Syllabus: Readings on Race, Racism, and Racial Violence*. Athens: University of Georgia Press, 2016.

Zeskind, Leonard. *Blood and Politics: The History of the White Nationalist Movement from the Margins to the Mainstream*. New York: Farrar, Straus and Giroux, 2009.

THE KU KLUX KLAN

Chalmers, David. *Backfire: How the Ku Klux Klan Helped the Civil Rights Movement*. Lanham: Rowman and Littlefield, 2003.

Chalmers, David. *Hooded Americanism: The History of the Ku Klux Klan*. Durham: Duke University Press, 1968.

Cunningham, David. *Klansville, U.S.A.: The Rise and Fall of the Civil Rights–Era Ku Klux Klan*. New York: Oxford University Press, 2012.

Leamer, Laurence. *The Lynching: The Epic Courtroom Battle that Brought Down the Klan*. New York: HarperCollins, 2016.

MacLean, Nancy. *Behind the Mask of Chivalry: The Making of the Second Ku Klux Klan*. New York: Oxford University Press, 1995.

Southern Poverty Law Center. *Ku Klux Klan: A History of Racism and Violence*, 6th ed. Montgomery: Southern Poverty Law Center, 2011.

CIVIL RIGHTS, MODERN SOUTH, AND GEORGIA

Bartley, Numan. *The Creation of Modern Georgia*. Athens: University of Georgia Press, 1983.

Belknap, Michal R. *Federal Law and Southern Order: Racial Violence and Constitutional Conflict in the Post-Brown South*. Athens: University of Georgia Press, 1987.

Carson, Clayborne. *The Eyes on the Prize: Civil Rights Reader: Documents, Speeches, and Firsthand Accounts from the Black Freedom Struggle, 1954–1990*. New York: Penguin Random House, 1991.

Cobb, James C. *The South and America since World War II*. New York: Oxford University Press, 2011.

Pratt, Robert A. *We Shall Not Be Moved: The Desegregation of the University of Georgia*. Athens: University of Georgia Press, 2002.

Tuck, Stephen. *Beyond Atlanta: The Struggle for Racial Equality in Georgia, 1940–1980*. Athens: University of Georgia, 2001.

Wexler, Laura. *Fire in a Canebrake: The Last Mass Lynching in America*. New York: Simon and Schuster, 2003.

CPSIA information can be obtained
at www.ICGtesting.com
Printed in the USA
LVOW03s2137280917
550421LV00002B/271/P